RULES for REBUILDERS

Steven Grant
Stanley Grant

ARCHWAY
PUBLISHING

Archway Publishing books may be ordered through booksellers or by contacting:

Archway Publishing
1663 Liberty Drive
Bloomington, IN 47403
www.archwaypublishing.com
1 (888) 242-5904

Because of the dynamic nature of the Internet, any web addresses or links contained in this book may have changed since publication and may no longer be valid. The views expressed in this work are solely those of the author and do not necessarily reflect the views of the publisher, and the publisher hereby disclaims any responsibility for them.

Any people depicted in stock imagery provided by Getty Images are models, and such images are being used for illustrative purposes only. Certain stock imagery © Getty Images.

ISBN: 978-1-4808-6717-8 (sc)
ISBN: 978-1-4808-6716-1 (hc)
ISBN: 978-1-4808-6718-5 (e)

Library of Congress Control Number: 2018912019

Print information available on the last page.

Archway Publishing rev. date: 10/29/2018

Contents

Introduction

If you are a Congressman, this book may not be for you.

If you bleed Team-Republican or Team-Democrat, this book may not be for you.

If you are thrilled and content with State and Federal bureaucracy, this book may not be for you.

If you think the mainstream media is truthful, trustworthy, and unbiased, this book may not be for you.

If you are interested only in sports or this weekend's sale at the mall, this book may not be for you.

If you love wealth and anonymity more than liberty, this book may not be for you.

If you spend more time playing video games than you do reading, this book may not be for you.

If you are a lukewarm Christian, content with church potlucks, this book may not be for you.

If you are a Pastor, consumed with only the church experience, this book may not be for you.

If you believe the United States of America is just fine the way it is, and YOU cannot do anything to change it anyway, this book may not be for you.

Give it to someone else.

This book is only for those who wish to water the tree of liberty; not those who wish to kill it, neglect it, or reshape it into a cute little bonsai.

This book is for those who are not drinking the Kool-Aid being poured out in America. We call it the "myth of cultural equivalency."

This book is for those who truly want to make America great again. For that to happen, true patriots will need to regain their heart of courage, and cultural voice.

- Not a voice that mirrors culture, but a voice that directs it.
- Not a voice that bows to political corruption, but a voice that takes it to task.
- Not a voice of surrender to enemies foreign and domestic, but a voice that says "not on my watch."
- Not a voice of bloviation, but a voice of humility and strength.
- Not a voice easily ignored by the establishment, but a voice that is feared by the establishment.

The book of Nehemiah (in the Bible) tells a story of a nation that instituted border security, reformed her economy, reclaimed her moral foundations, restructured education, instituted tariffs and trading policies that benefited herself, severed her ties with globalism, and expelled the enemies of the nation. Following these patterns, **"Rules for Rebuilders"** will lay out the blueprint to truly make America great again.

Our call to America

Albert Einstein is widely credited as saying "The definition of insanity is doing the same thing over and over again, but expecting different results." America has been in moral decline since the early 1920's. The last fifty years have revealed a decline in America's global leadership, our education systems, small business, and stable families (both financially and spiritually). Add to this, mountains of consumer and government debt, hundreds of thousands of regulations choking the life out of the citizenry, and untold "rights" awarded out of entitlement, based upon nothing foundational, only feelings and the "me" syndrome. That isn't exactly a formula for success. True freedom and liberty die slowly, but they always die when individuals become more important than the nation.

Can America be made great again? Yes! This is the heartbeat, the passion, of everyday Americans. Career politicians do not want that, but average Americans do. In spite of an established political machine that seeks to short circuit American sovereignty, exceptionalism, and liberty at every turn, there is still a mighty remnant that can turn this nation once again.

Can America be made great with our current direction and habits? Absolutely not! We have eagerly imported corruption, yet deported God from every segment of society. We aren't just talking about prayer in schools. We are talking about His blueprint. In the 1700's the average farmer read books like Blackstone's "*Commentaries on the Laws of England*" and Adam Smith's "*The Wealth of Nations.*" Today, lawyers avoid reading Blackstone, and economists avoid Smith's writings. Why? Because they are written at a level above most of their reading levels! Education was better in the 1700's than it is today. What changed? Why did we stray from the blueprint?

We will refer to Scripture verses regularly in this book. We encourage you to have your Bible handy so that the actual blueprint is in your hands. Do not just trust what we say. Study it. Verify it. Let it speak to you. You have a role to play in the days ahead.

There is a foundational Scripture found in Jeremiah 6:16:

"Thus saith the Lord, Stand ye in the ways, and see, and ask for the old ways, and see, and ask for the old paths, where is the good way, and walk therein, and ye shall have rest for your souls. But they said, We will not walk therein."

The blueprint we present to you is rooted in history, the past. We must look back in order to advance forward. In Jeremiah's time it was rejected, even though it offered a good life, rest for the soul, and strength to the nation. We must choose it now. Why? Because every time the blueprint is implemented, it works! This is the call to action; not just information. It is time to work the plan once again.

Saul Alinsky, an activist who wanted to separate America from the blueprint, once wrote a book he dedicated to satan himself. It was a subversive plan for revolution titled "Rules for Radicals." We give you "**Rules for Rebuilders**" as a blueprint for renewal. We unashamedly dedicate it to our Lord Jesus Christ, because in spite of what communists and progressives say, we are one nation under One God.

And the gates of hell shall not prevail.

Chapter 1 - Let's Get Real

Nehemiah 1

A group of businessmen from the across the nation have come to UN headquarters, to transact business and meet with global leaders. Upon hearing of their arrival, the highest ranking official from the State Department schedules time with them, to discuss national matters. When he asks about the state of the Union, this is their response.

The citizens are oppressed on practically every front. Border security is nonexistent. International terrorists have easy access; there are enemies within. Illegal aliens have free access to the nation's resources, and they enjoy more support than natural born citizens do, from the global community. The nation, once known as a shining city set on a hill and a beacon of liberty and prosperity to the world, is no longer a land of equal opportunity. Now, she is pillaged regularly for the purpose of redistributing her wealth. It is called taxation, but the people know it for what it has become; theft. Tariff and trade regulations have enriched global businesses, and closed factories and production centers across the land. The economy is designed to benefit only the elite. The middle class bears the brunt of the tax burden, and there are no controls on interest rates. Banks are not helping the little guy, they are taking everything from him, enslaving him to a lifelong yoke of credit, and just getting by.

For the younger generation, this is all they know. If they are lucky, they may have heard of the rule of law, but only as a theory. All they have seen is a President who rules by charisma and executive order, without any checks and balances. He's a well-tailored empty suit, but he sure talks pretty. What he says goes, and he is always in lock-step with the global community. The citizens really have nowhere to turn. The power brokers, pawns who have sold their souls for a seat at the table, do not represent the common man. The citizen's only recourse is to be subservient to the self-serving establishment. In short, national sovereignty has been all but destroyed, and the people are subject to the whims of foreigners who hate...yes, hate...their nation. Oh sure, people are eating, working, and getting an education. The nation is still referred to as one nation under God. But she no longer enjoys the liberty and prosperity that were bought and paid for with the blood and virtues of her forefathers.

Does this sound like America today?

This is actually a picture of Judah and Jerusalem during Nehemiah's time.

If it sounds all too familiar, it's time for Americans to get real, because it's not going away until we get serious about changing things. Nehemiah had a great job, and an excellent career. But the news from Jerusalem drove him to his knees. He actually cared about his nation more than his position, and he was determined to do something about it. He was determined to risk it all, even on pain of death. So if you can stomach the conversation, let's put first things first.

Making our nation great again does NOT begin with:

- Republicans winning the election.
- New entitlement programs.

- Universal health care, regardless of which narcissist it is named after.
- A new spending plan.
- Doing the same things over and over, with the same crop of leaders.

Today, there is too much business as usual, and not enough radical departure from the "norm." If you think that making America great again is all about electing Republicans, and coming up with some new spending plan, consider this; in spite of the pendulum swings, from one political party to the other, for decades, nothing has changed for the better. Instead, things have been getting worse, because both parties are committed to the status quo. Both parties are committed to globalism. Both parties are trending to the left. Both parties see themselves as elite, and the people as their subjects. They are interested in three things; consolidating power in their hands, removing it from yours, and getting reelected. "By the people, for the people" is not on their radar. The God we were founded under is only present in TV-ready sound-bites, or is used for closing speeches. Are you OK with this?

Tyranny by regulation

She escaped Cuba at the age of 27, coming to America with nothing but the clothes on her back and her birth certificate. Now a citizen of the United States, she has learned the language, carved out a niche in society, and started to build a business with her husband. At every turn in the road, they face regulation, taxation, and fees. If she plays the game according to the government rules, she may have a chance for a decent life. Her anger is palpable as she wades through piles of paperwork every day, and realizes that the communists and socialists in America seek to make her beloved United States just like the Cuban home she once fled so she might live in freedom.

Meanwhile In Manhattan

He is a sharply-dressed businessman, stepping off the commuter train to take his final steps into the office. He has an air about him that tells others he knows his way around town. Day after day this is his routine. He is good at his job, and makes a good deal of money. What most people don't know is the darkness that hounds him in secret. While the money comes into his hands, it also flows out. Liberally. The house payment for that home in Connecticut. School loans for his two children. And the taxes! The ever-increasing taxes! Nobody knows he is one step away from missing his water and electric bills. On the outside, his life is a success, but deep down, he knows things are week-to-week.

Organic raspberries

They had saved for years to buy eighty acres. His wife loves horses, and he loves the land. Now they have a mini-farm where they raise crops, enjoy the horses, and have built a home. Everywhere they turn, there is a new discovery. It might be the need for a high fence around the orchard, to keep the deer out. Or it might be the discovery that they can't sell their farm-grown raspberries without government permission. Actually, the permission comes in the form of a UPC code that has to be purchased. If it isn't purchased, the local stores cannot buy his berries. It is one of the many government regulations he has discovered, that controls his life and his property. There is always another tax, another fee. Nobody told him about this when they bought the land.

Welcome to Wal-Mart

She donned her bright blue vest and adjusted her smile. She hadn't planned to be a Wal-Mart greeter, but the retirement funds did not go as far as planned. The bond increase on the water filtration plant was "only" $20 per month for some, but for her it is three home-cooked meals. Then there is the surcharge for fuel for the trash trucks, the cost-of-living increase for the local council, and the hole in the roof. Her phone bill contains surcharges equaling thirty percent of the total. Her fixed income is really broken, and she has to find work. Welcome to the store...

False arrest

His family has lived in Southeast Colorado for decades, and he has built up his ranch and his livestock. It takes a lot of acres of sparse prairie grass to feed cattle, and his herds roam twenty thousand acres these days. His profit margins have been slim like many ranchers, and he was elated to hear that oil and mineral reserves lay beneath his soil. He was also stunned when local authorities arrested him on trumped-up charges, and put him in jail. He was freed weeks later and the charges were proven to be false, but since then he started to investigate the reasons behind the arrest. It soon became obvious that various governmental entities had also taken an interest in his oil and mineral rights. They want the land, and he is in the way.

So this is success

When they married, he "only" had forty-six thousand dollars in debt, including his student loans. His undergraduate degree is in English. She had brought nearly seventy thousand dollars of her own debt-load into the marriage, from credit cards, student loans, and a car. It isn't as much as many of her friends have accrued. Now they are married and live in a decent, two-bedroom apartment with their cat. She serves tables at a trendy restaurant, and he works at a local bank. Neither have been able to find work in their desired fields, and early newlywed life is difficult, mostly because of the financial burden. It will take years to dig out, but they are just taking life one day at a time.

Is this a picture of America?

Does this sound like the story of Jerusalem that Nehemiah heard? Can you relate to any of these people? They are real people, and their stories are true. This is how much of America lives today, and you probably know one or more of these people.

Do you care about the United States of America? Does your heart beat faster when you stand for the National Anthem or see the American flag? Do you long for the days when things were simpler, more honest, and cleaner? If so, this book is for you. The world around you may try to pigeonhole you under certain terms. Religious. Patriotic. Fanatic. Whatever! YOU can be one of the Nehemiahs of this generation, and *you* can make a difference. You are the ones that hold the nation together when it threatens to tear apart. And you cannot let America go, can you? What can we do?

We have to get real. If the foundations be destroyed, what can the righteous do? We have spent too much time dealing with the surface issues instead of getting to the root of the problem. It's like cleaning out cobwebs, but not killing the spider. Sure it feels good to feed the hungry, but they may be back tomorrow. Why? Because there is a deeper issue that remains unaddressed. Meanwhile, we feel good, even religious. We congratulate ourselves, pat ourselves on the back, and tell ourselves that things are well. But deep inside there is a knot in our stomach. Something isn't right. We have not been honest; honest with ourselves, with others, with God. Real solutions do not perpetuate the problems; they address them at the root.

Most of the issues in the paragraphs above deal with broken dreams, tyrannical governmental policies, regulatory control, and manipulation through economics and finance. They may not be your story, but our national debt IS your story, whether you like it or not. America's unfunded debt has been accrued by both Democrats and Republicans over the last several decades, so it's not a party problem. It's a moral issue when we continue stealing from future generations like we are. Let's break out our unfunded debt into five categories, bearing in mind that these are very rough estimates:

National Debt: $20 Trillion

This is the base amount the US is indebted for, just for operational expenses (military, infrastructure, food stamps, ESL programs, etc.). This is also the amount that you typically hear about through the mainstream media. It's not the only thing Joe Public is indebted for, but it's all you typically hear about. It's just the tip of the iceberg, but it's still significant. Your Portion: $61,000

Social Security: $160 Trillion

This is the amount owed to retirees that DOES NOT EXIST IN THE SYSTEM. Furthermore, there is no money in the Social Security fund. It has been stolen to pay for other government obligations, so it must be generated by someone as people get on Social Security. Where does the burden lie? On the back of Joe Public of course. Let us reiterate. What is the reason it is not in a bank somewhere as a fund for our retirees? Our government has used it for other things, yet cannot be prosecuted for the largest Ponzi scheme in history. Your Portion: $485,000

Medicaid, Medicare, and projected Obamacare: $90 Trillion

Once again, this is money committed to healthcare, at YOUR EXPENSE, that DOES NOT EXIST IN THE SYSTEM. Nor will it. Ever. We have outsourced America's manufacturing sector and taxed the business sector out of existence. We have increased

entitlement promises, but have undercut the base that funds en-
titlements like "free" healthcare. Your Portion: $273,000

Government / public pensions: $75 Trillion

General Motors is an example of a government union pension
fund. Any business or company taken over by the government
puts the taxpayer on the hook for their unfunded pension funds.
In addition, there are State and city pension funds, school districts, etc... As of this writing, California is $500 Billion in the
red on their State pension fund alone. Once again, the money
promised DOES NOT EXIST IN THE SYSTEM. Your Portion:
$227,000

If you have been keeping track, America's total unfunded debt
comes to around $345 Trillion, putting each CITIZEN on the
hook for roughly $1,045,454. Every baby born in an American
hospital today is born with that much debt, just because they are
an American. And the best part? Those who want us to bring in
millions of "refugees", are the same ones who want YOU to pay
for them with more debt! It's all brought to you, courtesy of 535
people in D.C., consisting of both Team-R and Team-D players.
So when we hear the politician promoting an economic plan that
increases our CUMULATIVE debt, it is insanity regardless of its
intended use. We need to get real.

Immigration

While it may be the economy that plagues many in America,
all of the issues in Nehemiah are the same as we face today.
Today there are seventeen thousand illegal children in the State of
Colorado, born to illegal aliens that live within the State. These illegals are demanding legal status for these "unfortunate children,"
whose average age is twenty five years old. Auto insurance rates in
Colorado are artificially inflated due to one significant problem.

Nearly thirty percent of the motorists on the road are uninsured. Many of these are illegal aliens, refugees, or low-income families.

The local school district is doing wonderful work, trying to educate the children in curricular basics. However, they are being hindered by the influx of refugees and others that have come into the area. (Keep in mind the fact that public education takes on everyone, no matter their status, income, or educational level.) Today there are sixty six primary languages being spoken in the local school district. These children require translators, cultural training, remediation, school breakfast and lunch programs, and a host of other specialized approaches. Who pays the bills?

At the national level, border security is a joke. The Obama dictatorship ruled by executive order, and gutted border security. This was done under the false pretense of loving our neighbor, while importing globalist, left-wing voters from a myriad of nations. Christian society was gutted as well. Marriage was taken from the church and given to the State in the name of homosexual "tolerance." Genders were stolen from science and DNA, and given to whatever the feeling of the day might be. The horrific term, "gender fluid" is no longer a joke. It's an identification for many fools, weirdos, and mentally unstable; yet it is lauded and applauded. Men that identify as women now compete in women's sports. Bathrooms are danger zones. Students are punished for referring to a "he" as a "she." This is the America we live in today.

Nehemiah did two things

Just two.

First he prayed. It wasn't a weak, insipid prayer that ended with a sigh and passive resignation. Something had to be done. The very existence of his nation was at stake. Nehemiah's sense of responsibility kicked in at a higher level, but he didn't know what he didn't know! Only God knew the details of His plan at that point. So Nehemiah started there.

He began by reminding God about what the Bible said about the nation. He didn't just pray once; he prayed repeatedly because this issue became such a burden. He knew Jerusalem was made for greatness, and the people were living below the level of their potential. In his agony, Nehemiah reminds us of a key element that we must reclaim.

God works through people who care

If you don't care about America, you might as well close this book. Now. If you are merely interested or curious, you may not have what it takes. Let's face it. There are many people in the United States today that would trade in their liberty for security. Every snowflake needs its safe space. This has been a problem since the Revolutionary War era. Samuel Adams, one of America's founding fathers said it best. *"If you love wealth greater than liberty, the tranquility of servitude greater than the animating contest for freedom, go home from us in peace. We seek not your counsel, nor your arms. Crouch down and lick the hand that feeds you; May your chains set lightly upon you, and may posterity forget that you were our countrymen."*

Jerusalem had been re-established many years before, but the powerful and the pitiful were doing nothing to change it, elevate it, or make it the great city it could be. The globalists and tyrants were more than happy to use the enslaved citizens as a cheap labor pool...a labor pool that was really smart. God had elevated the nation as the global leader in her prime, and the world community was just flat out jealous. Jealous enough to enslave her, and keep her under its thumb. The citizens did not think anyone cared. They also did not know what to do, or how they could stand up for themselves. They needed leadership that came from someone with a seasoned perspective.

Do you really mean...?

This led to Nehemiah's second revelation. As he considered the trouble Jerusalem faced, he got the sense that God was directing *him* to do something. Nehemiah had a great government job. He was the cupbearer to the king. He was involved with anti-terrorism and had a high security clearance. He was the king's informal advisor, and probably had a very comfortable living situation. The implications were huge. He would probably have to move. His job would be shifted to one that was dangerous and filled with political turmoil. Life would cease to be comfortable, and the outcome was uncertain at best. As Nehemiah prayed, he began to sense that this was God's direction. No mention is made of how Nehemiah felt about it.

Everybody, Somebody and Nobody

When everybody thinks that somebody is going to do something, in the end nobody does. Worse yet, instead of nobody, the globalists, wicked, and those with their own agendas step up. Homosexuals, progressives, communists, globalists, aliens and others have gladly filled roles in government, education, security, and the judicial realm. Fed by a steady diet of abandonment theology, Christians and patriots have often ignored or abandoned these areas for several reasons. Some have felt they were too unclean or dirty. Many have erroneously believed that God has no interest in national affairs. Others do not want to put in the hard work to earn a place of respect. Still others started to take a stand, but were shouted down or persecuted. They left to nurse their wounds, embittered, and willing to lose in peace, instead of remaining determined to stand and reclaim the nation.

Today, the reason many wicked men and women are in power is because many of us have not stepped up. You may be called to lay aside your retirement plans. You may have to volunteer at local levels, and put in many hours in seemingly worthless meetings, debating with progressives and communists in places like school board meetings, city council gatherings, and other boards. But you must answer this question: "How can I use my life to rebuild and reclaim this nation?" You are being called to lay aside your good life for one less predictable. You are called to live beyond your own self-gratification. Will the real Nehemiahs please stand? Jerusalem is broken, but the solution lies in the hands of Almighty God, and your personal sacrifice for this great nation.

If my people which are called by my name, shall humble themselves, and pray, and seek my face, and turn from their wicked ways; then will I hear from heaven, and will forgive their sin, and will heal their land. 2 Chronicles 7:14

Rule #1: Repent, and determine to become one nation under One God.

Questions:

- America is broken. Do you care?
- What drives you to your knees?
- What are **YOU** going to do about it?

Chapter 2 - Build the Wall

Nehemiah 2

Chapter 1 brings several truths to the forefront; America needs to get real, hit her knees, and then prepare to act. Rather than opting for a state of denial, Nehemiah embraced the (uncomfortable) facts, and the reasons why they were in their predicament. For decades, the nation had developed an appetite for globalism, and it opened the door to its unintended consequences. Globalism is *never* God's plan for one nation under God, yet Israel tried repeatedly throughout her history to be like all the other nations of the world. And it always...ALWAYS...brought about their judgement or downturn. Judah and Jerusalem had bottomed out on the cycle of nations; an eight-step process many nations have repeated throughout history.

The Cycle of Nations

1. From bondage to spiritual faith
2. From spiritual faith to great courage
3. From great courage to liberty
4. From liberty to abundance
5. From abundance to complacency
6. From complacency to apathy
7. From apathy to dependence
8. From dependence to bondage

America is in her own race to the bottom.

When one nation under God is in the throes of bondage, business as usual just doesn't cut it. Getting to the top of the cycle requires you to move from dependence and bondage, to spiritual faith and courage. That is a large leap to take, and always demands a radical departure from the norm. Real courage starts when you begin to see things for what they really are.

Leaving security and stability

Nehemiah was living his best life now. He held a high-level position with the king of the realm. He was personal friends with the king and queen. His circle of friends was large, and his lifestyle was comfortable. Life in Jerusalem was completely the opposite, and Nehemiah knew there was a cause greater than himself. This cause he presented to the king.

Nehemiah asked to resign. Give up everything! He asked to leave his position, move to Jerusalem, literally abandon the king and queen, lead the rebuilding effort, and effectively jeopardize everything in his life. His career, lifestyle, family, and future were at stake. Amazingly, the king said yes!

You may be reading this today, and want to do something great to reclaim this nation. If that is the case, then God is stirring you. But the call to rebuild and reclaim may cost you everything. You may need to relocate, and leave family and friends behind. You may be called to work with people, many of which dislike you, oppose you, and dishonor you. You may have to accept a lifestyle that is less than you and your family's desire. What is your price? What will you sacrifice to make America great again? John F. Kennedy once said, "ask not what your country can do for you, but what you can do for your country." Long before JFK said it, Nehemiah lived it. Are you willing to be next?

*"...I sought for a man among them, that should
make up the hedge, and stand in the gap before me
for the land, that I should not destroy it..."* Ezekiel
22:30.

Read the rest of that verse on your own. It's only four more
words, and it's not pretty. Never let it be said that God uttered
those words over America.

When the king approved his request, Nehemiah was so em-
boldened that he asked for more! Nehemiah was granted free lumber from the royal forest, and a personal security detail assembled
by the king. These were the two elements that Nehemiah brought
to the broken-down city of Jerusalem. When you seek to build
the kingdom, everything you need will be added to you. Life may
not always be comfortable, but it will be sufficient. Nehemiah had
the materials he needed, and protection God granted. God will
give us no less today.

The enemy within

When Nehemiah showed up in Jerusalem, he quickly became aware that not everyone approved of his arrival. Three of
the globalist governors in power were enraged. Why? Because
someone had come to "seek the welfare of the children of Israel."
There was no mention in the Bible of whether these governors
were Republican or Democrat. It didn't matter. Many people in
power on both teams are angered when someone comes to disrupt
their global agenda, and put the nation first. Ask yourself why,
no matter which party is in power, things don't really change for
middle- and lower-class America. When the Nehemiahs of the
nation begin to stand up, there will definitely be resistance from
the entrenched, established authorities. More on that later.

The assessment

Within three days of arrival, Nehemiah began to assess the city and the issues. But he didn't do it publicly; he assessed matters privately. He rose up at night, and took a few trusted men with him. He had told no one of his plans at this point. He circled the entire city, surveying it from every angle and perspective. There were no-go zones, where he could not pass, which he left alone initially. He was interested in gaining a clear understanding before he spoke.

One of the weaknesses of the "tea party movement" of 2009 lay in her impatience. The people were sincere, and had America's interests at heart, but most of them wanted quick and easy victories. They also did not want to pay the deeper price, suffer persecution, be separated from family and friends, endure the drudgery of long, boring political meetings (with the enemy, no less), and lose frequently on the way to victory. After all, the truth was obvious. Shouldn't we just adhere to it and move on? Yes. And no.

You see, the enemy has been in control, and he likes it that way. He doesn't intend to give up one inch of territory. We have failed to realize that the road to victory is a road of battle. Today the war is in ideology, media, education, and the social realm, but it is still a war. Many good patriots have abandoned those areas and conceded defeat already. We need modern day Nehemiahs to assess where things stand, and develop a plan of action. We must reclaim and rebuild, but it will take time, energy and commitment for the long-haul. Quick victories are often lost with the next battle.

As Nehemiah considered the state of his homeland, on the downside of the cycle, he realized the time was perfect for her to be rebuilt. In his address, he bypassed the nobles and the rulers. He went straight to the people. He told them of the plan, the blessing of the king, the lumber available, and the vision he carried. There was a micro plan starting to develop in Nehemiah's mind. From repentance...and a recognition of covenant relationship...comes a plan. How is Nehemiah's plan beginning to unfold?

Priority 1: Border Security!

In short; build the wall. If you read the account on your own, you'll see that Nehemiah even successfully negotiated to have another nation pay for it. This is the first of his endeavors to rebuild the nation. We discover the initiative is met immediately with the resistance of those who *WANTED* a broken border. This response of enemies both foreign and domestic makes sense, once you understand their reasoning. The way a globally-minded cabal weakens a sovereign nation's position of strength, is to maintain unrestricted access to it by way of open borders. America's weakness equals their strength. One of Mexico's former Presidents decried the idea of a wall, likening it to the Berlin Wall. In his words, "humanity made a grave error" when that wall was erected. He conveniently omits the truth that Mexico has its own wall on its southern border. And he fails to recognize that the Berlin Wall had a different purpose. It was designed to keep people in, to imprison them. America's wall is designed to keep criminals out, and keep our culture prosperous. Nehemiah faced the same challenge and the same arguments. He built the wall anyway.

Consider this quote from a speech given by Barack Obama a few years back:

> *"Long before America was even an idea, this land of plenty was home to many peoples: to British and French, to Dutch and Spanish, to Mexican, to countless Indian tribes. We all shared the same land. We didn't always get along. But over the centuries, what eventually bound us together – what made us all Americans – was not a matter of blood, it wasn't*

a matter of birth. It was faith and fidelity to the shared values that we all hold so dear. We hold these truths to be self-evident, that all men are created equal, endowed ("by their Creator" is left out of his statement) *with certain inalienable rights: life and liberty and the pursuit of happiness."*

When we read that, two points immediately come to mind that should be addressed.

1. Long before America was even an idea in the mind of man, it was an idea in the mind of God.

Everything must spin around God's idea for this nation, not man's ideas! Simply put, any political hack who seeks to redefine America in light of his own bias, is arrogant, and an enemy of the State. America is not the property of any political system or leader, who wishes to (re)define it in their image. That is satan's agenda though, so it doesn't surprise us when we see his minions attempt it themselves. They are just doing their father's bidding. The devil doesn't have the skill to build anything good on his own, so he always tries to redefine what God has blessed so that he can take the credit.

2. According to this narrative, everything on this Continent was peachy keen until the racist Europeans showed up and actually made something of it.

Prior to their arrival, North America was dreamland! If only those Saxon people would have embraced diversity, the group hug could have prevailed. Sigh. Perish the thought of them establishing a prevailing and dominant successful culture because of their ingenuity, administration, and work ethic.

Let us now correct the narrative: What made us all Americans was the Saxon conquest of the Continent. To name a few, we defeated tyrannical government, savages, Mexican usurpers, and even islam to become America. If you have doubts, look no further than the Barbary Wars under Thomas Jefferson. That was America's early battle with islamic terror. No group hugs, no coexist bumper stickers. Just winning.

It is not hard to see why today's "progressives" want America to be a concept without borders. Sorry, but we are still a nation WITH borders, and it's time to build the wall!

Globalism, God's way

Global borders are predefined in Deuteronomy 32:8-9. It reads *"When the Most High divided to the nations their inheritance, when he separated the sons of Adam, he set the bounds of the people according to the number of the children of Israel. For the LORD's portion is his people; Jacob is the lot of his inheritance."* This was enumerated around 1451 BC, we like to think of this as the Global Borders Act of 1451 BC. It clearly indicates that borders are created by God Himself, and colonial expansion will occur according to His plan.

His. Plan.

Early Americans called it "Manifest Destiny," and that label is actually correct. It was, and remains, God's destiny for this land to be the result of Anglo-European expansionism. Aztlan will not be rebuilt on our southern border, and there will not be any States leaving the Union. Why? This land is set up just as God wants it to be, and is possessed by who He wants to possess it. No matter who hates that, America was conceived in God's mind at the beginning of time, and is codified in the Global Borders Act of 1451 BC. In truth, God has been enacting this from the very creation of mankind as He moved people groups around the globe to their respective possessions. Because Anglo / Saxon peoples are the founding and prevailing culture of these United States, and God has ordained it to be so, they need to quit apologizing for being here. Manifest Destiny required many Anglo / Saxon nations to expand into territory already possessed by others, and they should be thankful for that.

Black privilege exists in Africa.

Asian privilege exists in Asia.

Mexican privilege exists in Mexico.

Muslim privilege exists in Iran, and other islamic countries.

Arab privilege exists in Saudi Arabia.

Frankly, we are OK with that. Let them have their territory, and let them give nation building their best effort (there). But why should Caucasian Americans be ashamed of being white, for the most part being Christian, for being here, and for building the greatest nation on earth?

If you are Caucasian, and suffer from white guilt, stop. Now. Do not apologize for winning the wars and possessing this land. Do not apologize for defeating savagery. Do not apologize for abolishing slavery with the blood of five hundred thousand of your sons. You have given minorities greater opportunity here than anything they could have in their home country, and you have not even asked for reparations from them in so doing. Do not apologize for the fact that you have built the greatest force for good that the world has ever seen. You have done it without global permission, so don't look to an underachieving global community for your validation. Do not apologize for the Pilgrims. Do not apologize for your Christian heritage. Celebrate Columbus Day, Independence Day, and Christmas. On Thanksgiving, give thanks to God, not socialists who want to destroy you. Do not apologize for being the only nation to place her feet on the moon. Do not apologize for building the greatest nation on earth.

Double down, and be proud of your heritage, even if others rage at it. This is not advocating the oppression of minority peoples or groups, it is merely celebrating and honoring the founding and prevailing culture of our great nation! As a Jew, Nehemiah rallied Jewish citizens, and built a wall to protect their culture. We can do the same, without fear, and without shame. The future does not belong to those who bow to the global system and allow them to lead. The future belongs to those who dictate the terms of liberty to the global system. While that may feel like a David vs. Goliath scenario, remember that Goliath did not stand a chance. With God's help David did the impossible, and we can too when we have His help. Do not apologize, and build the wall!

If you are a bleeding heart liberal Christian, who believes that borders no longer matter, let me direct you to some New Testament theology. The Global Borders Act of 1451 B.C. is upheld in Acts 17:26, which reads *"And (God) hath made of one blood all nations of men for to dwell on all the face of the earth, and (God) hath determined the times before appointed, and the bounds of their habitation..."*

Nothing changes in God's mind under the New Covenant, so you can put your borderless world pie-in-the-sky notions to rest. Borders were established by God in the Old Testament era, and He didn't change His mind when we got to the book of Matthew. Cast aside your silly notions that God took a Prozac at the end of Malachi, and suddenly changed His mind and mood towards everything from then on. You are wrong.

In one sense, Obama was right. Long before America was even an idea, this land of plenty was home to many peoples. But he's wrong to think it can remain under the administration of all peoples or global governance. They didn't build it. Long before it was home to many peoples, God determined the boundaries of this land and which people group would administer it. The Saxon people are the prevailing culture of America and are thus its overseers, its directors, with many people gathering under the umbrella built by them. Let's celebrate that!

The opposing mindset is precisely why Nehemiah's first priority was Border Security (build the wall). The border wall invokes immediate resistance by those who prefer God's people exist as a concept without borders. After all, this "one nation under God" concept is bad for diversity! If we actually believe that we are one nation under God, our belief presupposes an intolerance for celebrations of perversity. Believing as Christians means we may have to stand for values that are not popular around the globe, while standing against some values that are widely accepted. Oh the horrors of having a backbone. The goal of globalism is to nullify borders and weaken nations. If you undermine the land grants, as given by God, you can nullify God Himself. Then the State can BE God. At least that is what those preferring globalism would have you believe.

That is why globalists abhor the national exceptionalism that God promises to His people when they observe to do His commandments (see Deuteronomy 28). The blessings of God on a nation, and the elevation of that nation above other nations, validates God's Word. This is why globalists attack the "one nation under one God" concept with vengeance. To them, national sovereignty, strength, and blessing are enemies number one, two, and three. But this is why Nehemiah is such a good blueprint for America.

Make someone mad

If you want to "out" America's enemies, talk about securing our borders and strengthening our Judeo-Christian heritage. America's enemies start coming out of the woodwork in a hurry, and most likely they're within our borders. In Nehemiah's situation, Sanballat, Tobiah, and Geshem were not foreigners on the outside. *They were foreigners on the inside; traitors.* They were not seeking the nation's well-being. They were seeking to fundamentally transform Nehemiah's nation into their global image. They were operating against the nation (and God's Covenant) in the spirit of Judas. You remember Judas, right? The consummate insider, looking for an opportunity to betray the Christ-culture he had gained access to. Judas didn't destroy Christ, he sold himself to the agenda of those who wanted His destruction, and then opened up the door for them to invade.

You may think that there's no way these enemies of a free and sovereign nation could have any influence over the patriotic citizens of Judah. But as you will see, they were community organizers, organizing some of the citizens against their own culture. They had a degree of influence, resources, and power within the nation. Sanballat, Geshem, and Tobiah were top-notch in their efforts to undermine the culture and destroy any vestige of national exceptionalism. They were excellent speakers, charismatic even. These well-tailored empty suits spoke half-truths to the people, while betraying them with a kiss.

Reading Nehemiah, you will see there is a lot of opposition to this national rebirth taking place. There's a word describing a substantial hindrance to national renewal and sovereignty; it is the word "syncretism."

Syncretism

"Syncretism" is a noun meaning "the attempted reconciliation or union of different or opposing principles, practices, or parties, as in philosophy or religion." Today we call that "celebrating diversity." Cute little buzz words for national cancer. The patriots and rebuilders in Nehemiah's day had three groups opposing their efforts.

First, there were the syncretic Jews. They had remained in Judah and Jerusalem, yet had adopted the global agenda around them. Because of their oneness with the other nations, they had grown accustomed to professing God with their lips, yet worshipping idols. To them, the rebuilders were bigots who threatened to upend their way of life and displace their power.

Second, there were the heathen in Jerusalem. They had no desire or intention of allowing Judah to reclaim her sovereignty and God-given prominence in the region.

Finally, there were the historical enemies of Judah that surrounded the nation.

Pause and consider for a moment how that applies to America. We are a nation built on a Biblical framework. A majority in the US consider themselves to be Christians, yet less than 10% have a Biblical worldview. For the true American patriot, where does our opposition come from today? Syncretic citizens with soul ties to the global community and its values. Many may even classify themselves as Christians, yet have no Biblical worldview. These have aligned themselves with the global community and its agenda, and have grown accustomed to professing God with their lips while bowing to idols. Economic idols. Entertainment idols. Entitlement idols. The idols of power and prestige. Those who favor a return to Biblical values and national sovereignty are seen as bigots who don't demonstrate tolerance or supposed love toward the rest of the world. In Biblical terms, syncretic people are the foundation of the beast system (found in The Revelation), yet they don't even realize it. The feet of the image in Daniel 2:42-43 signifies the last-days emphasis on diversity and mixture, and GOD has stated that it will not work. Ever. Not then, not now.

Then there are the heathen in the US. They have no desire or intention of allowing us to reclaim our sovereignty and God-given prominence in the world. They disdain American exceptionalism, and seek for ways to subvert it.

Finally, we have the historical enemies that surround our nation. Some of them are at our borders (or what's left of them) right now. Some of them are within our borders, we just don't know it. Yet.

The walls are down

America truly is a land of "unwalled villages", and the task in front of us is twofold. Our task also follows a definite order:

1.   Rebuild our spiritual walls.

First and foremost is a national allegiance to Divine Providence and a return to a Biblical worldview.

2.   Rebuild our national walls, borders, sovereignty, strength.

We cannot PUT one before the other, and we cannot HAVE one without the other!

This is the snapshot of Nehemiah 1 and 2. Settle it in your minds right now that when we put this blueprint into motion, as we return to being one nation under God, *not everybody will like it* (cue the weeping and gnashing of teeth). Steel yourselves to that resistance now. God doesn't run His Kingdom based on global opinion polls, and America will not be governed by global opinion either. If you want to identify America's enemies, talk about securing our borders and strengthening our Judeo-Christian heritage. America's enemies will immediately balk at either proposition because they want us weak. This probably comes as no surprise, but some of them exist in Washington DC. In both parties. In your neighborhood. On TV. Even in your church. Remember, Sanballat and Tobiah were not foreigners on the outside, they were foreigners on the inside. They had not assimilated to the prevailing culture that God had vested in Judah, nor had they become defenders of it. Instead they were antagonists, who sought to oppress it and re-define the nation in a way subject to their world view. Such is the role of community organizers, using power for their own gain, organizing against a culture that Christ built. Subversives, traitors, serving their father lucifer.

As we move forward with our rules for rebuilders, you will discover that the enemies of national sovereignty and exceptionalism rely primarily on the tools of accusation, intimidation, offendedness, and weak or nonexistent defenses. Globalists paint rebuilders as the problem, when in reality the rebuilders are the solution. What Nehemiah stood for was painted as rebellion, when in reality Nehemiah's position was inspired by the heart of God. Apparently God's ways for a nation do not always garner the approval of the globally-minded!

> *Hate the evil, and love the good, and establish judgment in the gate: it may be that the LORD God of hosts will be gracious unto the remnant of Joseph.*
> Amos 5:15

Rule #2: Reject globalism, reject the status quo, and identify the enemies within America.

Questions:

- What do I need to leave to rebuild our nation?
- Am I a part of the problem, or the solution?
- How about my friends, my allies, my church?

Chapter 3 - Grab a Rock

Nehemiah 3

Kate

She was thirty-two years old, sweet, fun, and the joy of her family and friends. When the bullet tore through her aorta, she collapsed to the ground. Her father administered CPR on the spot, but she died in the hospital two hours later. The killer ran, tossing the stolen gun into San Francisco Bay. When police arrested him and located the weapon, they also discovered a horrible story. The murderer was an illegal alien that had been in and out of the country for nearly twenty-five years. He had committed numerous crimes, and loved preying on the citizens of the United States. The jury rendered a "not guilty" verdict to send a message to "bigots" who want criminal aliens deported.

Ryan

Ryan gasped in pain as his SUV lay on its side in the middle of the intersection, totaled and T-boned by a boozy man in a drunken stupor. The drunken perpetrator of this traffic violation was in the country illegally, and he was completely uninsured. Once deported, he found his way back into the same region within a matter of weeks. He did not care, and neither did the politicians. Business people loved his cheap labor, too. Ryan tried to use his insurance money to replace his totaled SUV, but the funds weren't sufficient. He now makes payments, and the illegal alien cannot be located so that suit can be brought for damages. Nearly one-third of the motorists are uninsured like him. Who foots the bill? You do.

Samuel

As a State Senator, Samuel was used to seeing large invoices cross his desk, but this one made his blood boil. It was a bill from various hospitals in his State, expecting reimbursement for women giving birth with no funds and no insurance. The common thread for these births was completely appalling. Each one was paid by the State for an illegal alien giving birth to a baby that would become their anchor to the nation. In less than one year, in one State, the bill totaled more than $19 million.

Refugees

The State director of refugee resettlement was in town, meeting with various social organizations. Present were the directors of clinics, dental programs, the local housing director and liaison to provide food benefits, translation services, and utility funding. The State had arbitrarily chosen a conservative section of the State to be populated with refugees, and their numbers had swelled to more than 11 thousand in a matter of years. The once conservative district was now swinging left in voting stance due to the influx of foreigners not loyal to American heritage or values, and the Public schools were inundated with foreign children. Sixty-six native languages were spoken in classrooms where English-only had been the historical norm, Low-income housing was strained, and every social program was under pressure. Pro-American curriculum in schools was replaced with awareness and socialization programs, and local citizens were often pressured to "understand"

and "embrace" the new arrivals. Still, the State offices continued their social engineering, designed to weaken the once conservative, constitutional region, and change it into a pro-globalist enclave.

These stories are real. The issues continue every day, every week, every month. Washington, D.C. has not changed it, and will not change it. Never forget; "cannot" is different than "will not," and D.C. is operating from a "will not" position. Somebody must do something. That somebody...is you.

You say we don't need a wall? Wrong!

Border security was job number one in Nehemiah. Border security must become our first priority here, too. America *must* reclaim and defend her borders if she is to remain a great nation. Boundaries matter, and if the drain on society doesn't convince you of that, you are part of the problem. The physical and visible work begins with building a wall, but America must reclaim her spiritual and sociological borders as well. The real work begins in the heart and soul. Hollywood has power in society because you let them have it. Overpaid athletes dominate conversation because you have idolized them. We have demonized God and deified glamor, entertainment, sports and wealth. These idols must fall. We must rebuild values, morality, and virtue, in order to have national security and stability. Do not let Hollywood or mainstream media tell you otherwise. And *never* let them tell you that you must acquiesce to the status quo.

In Nehemiah's day, the people were inspired by the vision to restore the nation to its *former* glory. They did not mobilize to redefine it as progressives. They did not mobilize to open its borders even more, and embrace the myth of cultural equivalency. They mobilized to restore their nation as reformers. They mobilized as nationalists, under God. They mobilized to stand against globalism, not embrace it. Entire families rose up with a vision of returning to the old paths, and began to build the portion of wall that was right out their own front door.

Today, we must do the same. One may work on reclaiming education; another, business. Law, economics, education, foreign policy, etc., are all in need of reformation. The key element that everyone must seize is this; *business as usual is not acceptable anymore.* Chapter 3 of Nehemiah shows that practically everyone was engaged in restoring the nation. Nehemiah may have been a catalyst to get the ball rolling, but the people rose up with a mind to work. God Himself was their general contractor; their overseer. When they started, their nation was completely overrun with illegal aliens, and the lack of border security made them wholly subject to global whims. Maintaining and coping with the status quo was (temporarily) reality, but the mindset was no longer welcome. The people made the quality decision to restore, not just merely cope with a broken mess. They did it one individual, one family at a time. Don't you think it's time for all Americans to make that same decision?

But I don't feel like it!

Would you walk away from an untended fire, surrounded by pine trees and needles? No! But most of you, the readers, have walked away from tending government. People complain all the time about how government is broken, but it really works quite well. The system is working for those that are involved.

Go back and reread that last line again. And again! And again!

So what's the problem? The problem is that it is emotionally convenient to sit and complain, and do nothing. Too many people are too comfortable living with the walls down, comfortable with illusions of security. We do not supervise government, so it no longer fears "we the people." Most patriots are more than happy to vote every 4 years or so, complain frequently, make an occasional call to some politician they know, and otherwise completely avoid government. That is horrible stewardship! No wonder the liberals, globalists and communists have taken over! We have abandoned our governmental responsibility! The apostles Peter and Paul didn't run from government; they spoke directly to it! Other early church leaders did the same thing with boldness that got them killed! It's your turn now, to put your neck on the line. Does any of the following describe you?

- Too many Christians attend and fund churches that are preaching weak, insipid messages because they have attended there for years. They like the children's program, or are just too lazy to confront the leadership or leave.
- Too many patriots are happier complaining to their friends over coffee about how bad America is, but they don't bother to attend city council meetings, or put their reputations on the line.
- Too many business leaders don't want to risk their profits by putting themselves into the fight. Self and greed are their chief motivators, and they have forgotten that America's forefathers pledged their lives, fortunes and sacred honor for our sovereignty and liberty.

If you really want a job that suits lazy desires, run for Congress. Your job will consist of conducting endless investigations into the other "side" while never reaching any conclusions. You won't legislate much, and you will litigate a lot. When you do legislate, you will have the opportunity to write legislation designed to make you rich, and favor the global influences that leach off of the American system. You will get paid handsomely to do so, and after a long day of posturing for the cameras and your voter base, you can all do dinner together at the country club. And you will earn the disdain of the new nation that is rebuilt.

Changing America is not a feeling, it's a decision. It's a decision that Nehemiah made in his day, and it's a decision the people had to make right along with him for national transformation to take place. At what point will Americans realize that it's almost *pitchforks and lanterns* time? When you get involved in government, you begin to build the wall. You change the face of the game. You have a voice!

The city council race

The county clerk recently sent out nearly 130,000 ballots to registered voters in a city in Northern Colorado. At stake were the seats in the city council, the local school board, and the mayor's office. Local issues included: the building of a mosque; the approval of the Bible being taught as an elective class in high school, use of taxpayer dollars to fund private business, and very expensive bond issues.

The four members of the school board were unopposed, and automatically won because they were interested. The mayor was hand-picked by his predecessor with little to no opposition. Several extreme, left-wing liberals ran for city council against weak conservative contestants. In the end, the total number of ballots returned were less than 20,000 in number! The very reason that evil prevailed in the election, at every level, IN A CONSERVATIVE COUNTY, was because the patriots and conservatives did not get involved! They could have won handily, but chose not to engage in politics and government.

But politics are dirty

Wall building is always dirty, messy work. If you want to rebuild America, you are going to have to do it anyway.

- If you will be involved in rebuildi[...]
  lose frequently, until you win. Y[...]
  against losing, and press on anyw[...]
- If you want to rebuild America, [...]
  talent and money. The price is w[...]
- If you want to rebuild America, you mu[...]
  have enemies, and be willing to fight. No more Mr. Nice
  Guy. We are fighting for the soul of a nation, and it is war.

Many patriots do not understand that they are already at war. Progressives know it, and they know that if something is worth fighting for, it's worth fighting dirty for. They have no moral problem with changing the rules in the middle of the game, if it benefits themselves. The contest may begin as a football game, but if progressives are losing, they will quickly change it to a baseball game. Honorable people are slow to pick up on that kind of deceit, because we play fair. In this contest for liberty, don't get caught bringing a knife to a gunfight.

Just remember that a physical war is about killing people and breaking things. It is not neat, clean, or pretty. In the war for the heart and soul of our nation, it is no different. We must engage the established machine with a ruthlessness that may not come easy. Perhaps it is time for American patriots to lower the white flag, take the gloves off, quit responding to fake rules imposed by the enemies of liberty, and begin to impose the rules ourselves. If America is worth fighting for, it's worth fighting dirty for.

When dealing with politicians

Many of you already have an issue that is on your heart that is critical to the restoration of America. If you do nothing, America will continue to slide downhill. If you commit yourself to the building process, America can be changed.

Do you want the government to slash spending, and end social programs?

- Do you support the right to keep and bear arms?
- Do you want your religious liberties to be enforced?
- Do you want lower taxes?
- Do you want to slash regulation?
- Do you want to end abortion?
- Do you want to transform education?
- Do you want to stop illegal immigration?
- Do you want to cut off the flow of muslims into America?

You must be the one to champion your cause. You must be the one to own the fight. Get a rock, and find your place on the wall!

Nothing new under the sun

America has been here before, but it was a long time ago. Consider the words of Thomas Jefferson, captured in the Declaration of Independence:

> *"When in the Course of human events it becomes necessary for one people to dissolve the political bands which have connected them with another and to assume among the powers of the earth, the separate and equal station to which the Laws of Nature and of Nature's God entitle them, a decent respect to the opinions of mankind requires that they should declare the causes which impel them to the separation.*
>
> *We hold these truths to be self-evident, that all men are created equal, that they are endowed by their Creator with certain unalienable Rights, that among these are Life, Liberty and the pursuit of Happiness. — That to secure these rights, Governments are*

instituted among Men, deriving their just powers from the consent of the governed, — That whenever any Form of Government becomes destructive of these ends, it is the Right of the People to alter or to abolish it, and to institute new Government, laying its foundation on such principles and organizing its powers in such form, as to them shall seem most likely to effect their Safety and Happiness. Prudence, indeed, will dictate that Governments long established should not be changed for light and transient causes; and accordingly all experience hath shewn that mankind are more disposed to suffer, while evils are sufferable than to right themselves by abolishing the forms to which they are accustomed. But when a long train of abuses and usurpations, pursuing invariably the same Object evinces a design to reduce them under absolute Despotism, it is their right, it is their duty, to throw off such Government..."

Read it again.

And again!

Let it soak in, and think of its implications if we apply it in real time.

Do you think we are discussing light and transient causes? Americans had a revolution because of a tax on tea! What would our founders say today if they looked at the fees, surcharges, taxes, and levies added to your phone bill? What would they say about mosques being built on our soil? When Congressional approval ratings rank consistently in single digits, don't you think it's time for wholesale change? Have the drugs of professional sports and "retail therapy" dulled your mind to the point that you are useless? Are you lazy? Don't you think there is sufficient cause to cast off globalism, and make a return to American exceptionalism?

Restoration awaits. Border security awaits. American exceptionalism awaits. It's waiting on you. It's waiting on us.

We will discuss tactics further on in the book, but chapter 3 of Nehemiah illustrates two simple truths;

1. The people had had enough, and…
2. They were determined to get involved.

All of them. National misery continues as long as we will let it endure. Are you done yet, or do you secretly like the life of ease and self-indulgence? That is the *real* enemy within America, and it may live in you. Life will get worse in our nation until you make the change inside your heart. There is a military term denoting a 180 degree reversal of direction. It's called repentance, and we need to apply it. Now.

You don't need more

You don't need something more. You need to start to work with what exists today. Our forefathers had axes, ox-drawn wagons, and work-worn hands, yet they forged a civilized society in the wilderness. We have what we need. We just need to get to work. The people had everything they needed to rebuild the walls of Jerusalem. Nehemiah had secured the lumber for the gates and other items, but the rest of the material lay in the rubble. One man's trash; patriot's treasure. We have what we need.

- God.
- The Bible.
- Our Constitution.
- Our national history.

We know what worked before. We must build it again.

The people that started to build are listed by name and family in Nehemiah chapter 3. They were priests, merchants, pharmacists (yes, really), and goldsmiths. Heroes all. Everyone in society now had to grab a rock (a really big one), and figure out how to get that rock out of the pile of rubble and make it a viable part of the wall. Everyone stepped out of their comfort zone to make it work.

Almost everyone.

What about the ones that do not help?

There were two groups in Nehemiah that did not help build the wall.

One was called the "nobles of Tekoa." They were elitists with status and standing as "leaders" in the community. Simply put, they were politicians, more closely aligned with the problems, than the solutions. We are left to speculate why, but it is probably not a stretch to believe that engaging in real solutions could have cost them their cushy lives. They were beneficiaries of the status quo, and had no reason to change it. It is nice to be revered for doing nothing, and this wall idea changed everything. A change in the status quo could mean that they might be held accountable to the people, and their connections to any special interest groups would become null and void.

The second group was the globalist segment of the population of Jerusalem. They mocked Nehemiah and the wall builders, and they refused to help. The work of restoration would be in the hands of the average citizen, who would be reviled by the establishment. If you won't work, which group do you choose to identify with?

The builders, however, refused to let the mockers and the elite influence their work. They built anyway. **When people mock, persecute, or refuse to help, do it anyway**. Today, Jerusalem's walls are in place because citizens aligned with a vision of restoration, in opposition to the globalist cabal. What a tribute to the patriots in Nehemiah's time!

Where do we begin?

Every area of life and society needs to be rebuilt right now. Education is broken. The church is no longer salt and light. It is trying to be sugar, and is too busy taking its cultural image from society. Government is self-serving. Small business is trying to survive, while big business cozies up to their friends in government to perpetuate their greed and oppression. The justice system is now just a legal system. Interpreted, many laws are on the books to "legalize" certain practices; but it does not make them just, fair, or applicable to all. The FBI and IRS have been weaponized by the Left. It is all broken! So we must lay aside the idols of entertainment and self-indulgence. We, you, all of us must start to rebuild society now. The easiest thing to do is pick the spot closest to you, and get to work. Just like in Nehemiah's day, your section to rebuild is the closest section to you.

For instance, if your passion is reclaiming education, you must start to study what education was like when it was successful. You must understand how the Bible and New England Primer made America great. You must discover the fabric of Christianity in public education. You must discern how simple classrooms in the wilderness of the colonies taught advanced classes in math, literature, language, and Christian worldviews. Then you must insert yourself into the muck of today's educational swamp to root out evil, pull down the things that are destroying the children, and begin to rebuild and replace. It may take you your entire life to gain a few victories, but you must commit to rebuild that section of the wall.

The walls already have a foundation

When Nehemiah rebuilt the wall in Jerusalem, the foundation was already there. In fact, it had been built centuries before. The last person to expand and strengthen the foundations of Jerusalem had been king Uzziah, more than 150 years before the fall of the city. Everything Judah built from that point forward was built upon the foundation laid by somebody else. A foundation ordained by God. They could pick their rock. They could pick their spot. They could not pick their foundation. It had already been laid by their forefathers. The same holds true for America.

America's foundation was, and is, rock-solid. The U.S. Constitution has remained intact, and governed America to greatness since its inception. In contrast, the godless government of France has endured no less than fifteen seismic shifts during the same time period. Our governing documents (e.g., the Mayflower Compact, the Declaration of Independence, the Constitution and the Bill of Rights) are still in place even though they are frequently ignored. Ignored by those who should revere them. Furthermore, this may come as a news flash to the uninformed; they are not living documents. They are unchanging, as solid as bedrock. America has a great foundation to build upon, even if it is currently buried under the rubble.

If we were to look back 150 years, we would see a significantly different United States of America.

- The Federal government was quite small, and limited in scope.
- Guns were everywhere. Everyone had them, and used them for hunting, defense, and sport.
- Money was wealth-based instead of debt-based; gold and silver backed the economy.

- Charity was a private enterprise. Government gave no handouts.
- The Bible and the New England Primer were the primary textbooks in all public schools.
- Marriage and divorce were enforced by the church; not the State.
- Blue laws, blasphemy laws, capital punishment and other strict moral laws were respected and enforced.
- Criminals were dealt with swiftly.
- Justice was meted out by juries, hangings and stern judges.
- Juries weighed the laws and the defendant in the courtroom.
- The Federal Reserve Bank did not exist.
- The IRS did not exist.
- Property taxes were limited.
- Most of America was prosperous, even wealthy by comparison to the rest of the world.

Any wall building efforts must be laid on a foundation of what God will bless, not just what we want Him to bless. There is a difference. We can sing "God Bless America" until we are blue in the face, but until we understand the difference between the two, it's just a pretty song. Pretty songs won't change America, but building on a right foundation will. It's time to build on this foundation.

Walls need strong materials

America must not be built upon opinions, feelings, or secular doctrines. This is the garbage that has sent America into a tailspin. The progressives of today have socially-engineered America away from morality, God, the Bible, and a Christian foundation. Instead they have chosen globalism, secularism, socialism, communism, atheism, and humanism as their building blocks. This wall cannot stand. Never has, never will.

You may think that we are more "enlightened," or more "wise" than those who came before us. Really? They built pyramids, formed governments, established constitutions, and turned the wilderness into civil societies. It is true that the average American farmer only had an 8th grade education, but he could read and discuss at length the books in his library. The most popular studies were the 1599 Geneva Bible with extensive commentary, Blackstone's Commentaries on English Law, and Christian philosopher Adam Smith's foundation for free-market capitalism, the "Wealth of Nations." Can you equal their level today?

Simply put, the materials we build with must be overtly Judeo-Christian in structure and morals, and every law and statute in the land must snap to the common law of Scripture.

Walls need wall-builders

Nehemiah did not build the wall by himself. Everybody helped. If you have read this far, you understand your commission. Your role is not optional; it is mandatory. Put down the remote, shut off the computer, and start rebuilding society. Your children do not need that peewee football game or dance class as much as you think. You need to be at city council meetings, or better yet, sit on the council itself. You need to attend school board sessions and other endless, boring governmental gatherings. Why? Because in your absence, others fill those roles. Government is working for them, by the way. They dared to insert themselves into the vacuum left by lazy, complaining Americans that want to do nothing and yet reap huge rewards. You are being called back into the fight.

It is true that you have representative government, but you must watch your elected official. You must let them know you are there, and you care how they vote. Every time. You must hold them accountable, and inflict pain when they are poor public servants. And you must elevate your care for wall-building above every other concern except for the fundamentals of faith and family in your life. If not you, then who? If not now, when?

Walls need builders that cooperate with each other

If you want to rebuild America, you are going to have to learn to work with others around you. No, you probably aren't going to be the boss. Yes, you can have your own section of the wall to build, but you are going to have to support the wall builders on both sides of you, too. Your wall must connect to theirs, or you will end up leaving a gap for the enemy to enter. Your pride and ego must be laid aside for the sake of building the wall and making it a powerful defense against the enemy.

Everybody in Nehemiah's day picked a place to build. The foundation was laid for them by previous generations. The rocks for the wall were already there, in the piles of rubble. The builders all picked a place to build that was close to their home or business. Then they all built together. Many well-intentioned people want to play the role of Nehemiah and direct the operation. America doesn't need more directors; America needs builders. The general contractor is God, the master-builder is Nehemiah, and the workers are you and me. Builders figure out a way to build, even though construction may not be their skill. Builders will also join their segment of the wall to those on either side, to build something greater than a tower. Independent building without cooperation, builds nothing more than a pile of rocks. You must learn to cooperate with people that are not exactly like you, yet want the same outcome. Don't tear them down; build them up. Their work is just as important as yours. Many times the globalists are more united in their hatred, while those that believe in America are proud, fragmented, and divided. This must change.

When we begin

When you start to rebuild America, you will encounter resistance from several sides. First, the work is hard. The lazy did not build America, and they will not reclaim her in this day. Strengthen your hands for the job. Your work will be rewarded. Secondly, the globalists will oppose you. Today many of these enemies of liberty are found in education, government, churches, business and even in your circle of acquaintances. You must understand some of their tactics and how they operate so that you can know how to successfully rebuild America despite their opposition.

How globalists work

Globalists want to keep you out of *their domain*. Many of them think they are more enlightened than you. They want to keep you in your *little* life, while they pull the strings and control everything around you. They want to tell you whether or not you have "liberty," instead of acknowledging that your rights and liberty come from Almighty God, directly to you. When their talking heads are speaking on television or radio and you listen, they win. When they import people from other nations and give them government programs, they win. When liberals attend government meetings and speak up, and you don't, they win. When they act like they own the nation, and all you do is complain, they win. In every one of these cases, you lose! It's time to change that paradigm.

We need walls

The reason government is working the way it is today, is because we let it happen.

> *"He that has no rule over his own spirit is like*
> *a city that is broken down, and without walls."*
> Proverbs 28:28

We have failed to govern ourselves. We want to live our best lives now, instead of attending a city council meeting. We want the good life instead of sacrificing. Our cities are decaying, many of our States are in trouble. Our nation needs literal walls, moral walls, and wisdom in government. There is no better time than now, to consider your role and prepare to apply what you are learning. Start. Now. Who will build it? You will. Grab a rock. You are going to need it, as you will discover in the next chapter.

> *Also I heard the voice of the Lord, saying, Whom*
> *shall I send, and who will go for us? Then said I,*
> *Here am I; send me.* Isaiah 6:8

Rule #3: Embrace nationalism under God, get involved building that wall.

Questions:

- Where is your place on the wall? What is your mission?
- Who will you join with, to build a wall and not just an agenda?
- What must you *subtract* from life, to rebuild and reclaim America?
- What is the legacy you want to leave behind?

Chapter 4 - God, Guts and Guns

Nehemiah 4

When you decide to rebuild and reclaim America, you will make enemies. *This is because you are right; not wrong.* The best people in the world have enemies, while many tyrants are adored. Che Guevara was a vicious murderer, and his picture is on the t-shirts of the left. Stupid college students wear his brand, not caring how evil he was. They are truthophobic. Fidel Castro has been adored by many, and he was a thief and a communist tyrant. Many God-fearing patriots are hated and demonized. They are called racist, homophobic, and a host of other names. They are the real heroes, and they are hated for standing for America. Which side do you choose?

You must steel your mind, your emotions, and your family to difficulty. You must learn to do hard things, and ignore the voices on the outside. You will be thought unchristian, uncharitable, and evil. It is a time when evil is called good, and good is called evil, so there is no sense adjusting to their definitions and labels. Keep calm and carry on.

When the wall was being built and border security was being implemented, it was the globalists that became enraged. They started with a war of words. Today, the mainstream media is frequently on the side of wrong and evil. They are the wordsmiths, the pawns of the globalists and the elite. If you believe them, you will lose. If you ignore them, you will win. Listen to them just enough to understand their agenda. Then keep on building.

The church is frequently on the wrong side as well. They try to be nicer than Jesus, and want to play kissy-face with evil. It's all about appearances, not reality. Jesus talked about building Kingdom. We should, too. Christians need to put teeth into government again, by inserting the morals and values found in the Bible; all sixty six books of the Bible. But the greatest danger in media, the church, education, and other areas of society, are the globalists.

Globalists have a dream

In Nehemiah's day, the globalists raised their ugly heads early in the rebuilding process, and they did it again in chapter 4. The "one nation under God" idea was verbally attacked and threatened by thugs who didn't like it. Not only that, they appealed to foreign nations for support, to undermine the work of the patriots. These globalists rabidly opposed the colonial nature of the nation's expansion, which had been ordered by God. Globalists hated the national exceptionalism of Israel then. They hate America's national exceptionalism and colonial roots today.

So what is the globalist dream for these United States? We all know it is NOT the American dream as conceived by our forefathers.

- Other nations had monarchies. America had a Constitution established on the framework of the Bible.
- America's founders believed the nation was a "new order for the ages"...the new Israel.
- They believed in colonialism from sea to shining sea.

- President James Polk was well known for advancing America's "manifest destiny."
- A half-century after America's founding, Alexis de Tocqueville wrote of America as creating "a distinct species of mankind."

This speaks of American exceptionalism...something progressives and globalists detest. They go to great lengths to communicate to the world community that we are just one of them, and we are no more unique or exceptional that any other country. It's the myth of global equivalency, and the gullible drink the Kool-Aid.

America was made to be exceptional, and it's time we stop apologizing for being the exceptional nation that we are! America is so great, that even those who hate it refuse to leave. Our exceptionalism puts us in direct contradiction with every other nation of the world. At some point, it will put us in direct conflict with every other nation of the world.

The globalists wrote it down

In Barack Obama's book *"Dreams from My Father,"* he clearly exposes how a globalist thinks, and what their goals are for America. Obama's position was that rich countries of the West got rich by invading, occupying and looting poor countries in Asia, Africa, and South America. As an anti-colonialist, he believed that even when countries secure political independence, they remain economically dependent on their former "captors." These nations continue to be manipulated from abroad by corporate and governmental elite. The playing field must be leveled. What is the solution? The only obvious one presented and embraced is to resist and overthrow the "oppressors" (that being nations like America).

Globalists believe every nation they perceive as being "colonialist" must first be weakened. How? Through open borders, lax social policy that guarantees programs for all, and redistribution of its wealth. In fact, Barack Obama's father proposed a horrific solution for America. He wanted the government to confiscate private land, and raise taxes with NO UPPER LIMIT. In his own words, he insisted that *"theoretically there is nothing that can stop the government from taxing 100% of income so long as the people get benefits from the government commensurate with their income which is taxed."*

Let that sink in. A socialist/globalist/communist advocating up to a 100% tax on your income. This is the dream of the globalists for America, for you, and for your children. They are through debating, and are now intent on bringing this about. They will demonize you. They will riot in the streets. They will use every position of authority to make sure this happens! Do you understand how committed they are? Do you understand how serious this is?

It really is that serious

Why do we bring this up here?

- When policy becomes contrary to America's manifest destiny...
- When policy seeks to undermine our sovereignty, power, independence, and wealth...
- When policy attacks our being one nation under God in the way that He has ordained...

That policy and ITS LEADERS must be identified as the enemy within!

Nehemiah had them in his day, and we have them in ours.

To the globalist then, Israel was imperialism on a rampage. To the globalist today, America is imperialism on a rampage. Same story, different location. Same spirit behind it too.

This is why they want open borders, control over the economy, control over the industrial complex, unlimited power to tax, the power to control industry through "climate change", and control over the health industry. Globalists want everything under their control so they can neuter American strength and re-distribute its resources to whomsoever they wish.

It explains why they want people who are already paying close to 50% of their income in taxes, to pay even more. After all, not even a 100% tax is unreasonable to achieve the tyrant's dream of "social justice" and equality. It even explains why they want open borders, and why they present islam as a "religion of peace", equal to Christianity.

It even explains why Barack Obama wanted NASA to retool itself to be an agency that would improve relations around the muslim world. Yes, you heard that right. NASA's director was instructed by the President himself to "...*find a way to reach out to the Muslim world and engage much more with dominantly Muslim nations to help them feel good about their historic contribution to science and math and engineering.*" You know, one small step for man, one giant leap for islam.

One small step for man...and one giant leap for mankind... is interpreted as American exceptionalism and dominance to the anti colonial mind, and must be apologized for. The pea brains of the enemy within can't stand for national exceptionalism, and they dream of our national demise. Yet in spite of their grandiose dreams, globalists also have a nightmare.

Globalists have a nightmare

When globalists are trying to take over a nation, they always stack the deck. They pass new laws, and appoint lawless judges that will enforce their agenda. It happened in Nehemiah's day, it happens today. In particular, there's one cultural dynamic they

NEED in order to ultimately prevail, to conquer. It is something the enemy within is working to impose on us at this very moment.

It is the disarmament of we the people.

What is the nightmare scenario for the enemy within? It is people clinging to guns and religion! Simply put, it is the citizen's unalienable RIGHT to keep and bear arms, thus enabling them to wage war against the enemies of liberty. In Nehemiah's day, the outcome resulted in large degree on the people being armed... both with a weapon, and a willingness to use it if necessary. Please note that Nehemiah did not require that all swords be registered, and you did not need a permit to carry one. God's Word to rebuild was liberty's soul, but the sword was liberty's teeth.

On December 20, 1787, Founding Father Thomas Jefferson wrote a letter to fellow founder James Madison. In that letter he said this, *"What country can preserve its liberties if their rulers are not warned from time to time that their people preserve the spirit of resistance. Let them take arms."*

This is the power that keeps tyranny in check.

Reason or force

Human beings only have two ways to deal with one another: reason and force. If you want me to do something for you, you have a choice of either convincing me via argument, or to force me to do your bidding under threat of force. Every human interaction falls into one of those two categories, without exception. Reason or force!

In a truly moral and civilized society, people exclusively interact through persuasion...force has no place as a valid method of social interaction. When confronted with an enemy the only thing that removes force from the menu is an equal or greater force.

In Nehemiah's day the people used swords to keep the peace. In today's world, we do not use swords. We keep the peace with firearms. That may sound like a paradox, but it's not. When I carry a gun, you cannot deal with me by force. You must use reason to try and persuade me, because I have a way to negate your threat or employment of force.

We have famous examples from the last century of the firearm being a deterrent to global invasion. General Yamamoto did not invade America because he said there would be a "rifle behind every blade of grass." Hitler did not invade Switzerland, even though he had twice their manpower. His reason? Switzerland informed him that each of their people would just have to shoot twice. We want peace, but it must be peace through superior firepower.

Remember, Jesus didn't say "Blessed are the pacifists", He said "Blessed are the peacemakers", and sometimes the price of peace is war. We must be able and willing to pay that price when the time comes.

Liberty's teeth

The Bible will always be liberty's soul, but in modern times, the firearm has been liberty's teeth. The gun is the only personal weapon that puts a 100-pound woman on equal footing with a 220-pound mugger. It puts a 75-year old retiree on equal footing with a 19-year old gang banger. It puts a single guy on equal footing with a carload of drunk guys with baseball bats.

The gun removes the disparity in physical strength, size, or numbers between a potential attacker and a defender. The gun is the only weapon that's as lethal in the hands of a secretary as it is in the hands of a weightlifter.

In addition, a gun will do EXACTLY as you say.

- It won't argue back, and it won't act on its own accord.
- If you tell it to stay put, it will stay put.
- If you tell it to fire, it will fire.
- The bullet goes precisely where you point it.

It does no more...and no less...than what you instruct it to do.

There are plenty of people who consider the gun as a SOURCE of evil. Some people think we'd be more civilized if all guns were removed from society, simply because bad guys use them to be bad. It goes without saying that things are much easier for bad guys if their potential victims are disarmed, either by choice or by legislative tyrants. That argument has no validity when a thug's potential victims are armed...and the weapons are used in self-defense. That shows that guns aren't the SOURCE of either good OR evil...they're just a tool to extend one or the other. A mugger can only make victims in a society where the State has granted him a force monopoly.

A word to Christians

You may wish to coexist, to get along, to live in peace and to be in harmony with your fellow man. You may even wonder where the right to keep and bear arms comes from. Is it merely a political topic? Or are its roots found in Scripture? It may surprise some, but throughout the Bible God was pro-conquering, pro-self-defense, and pro-national security. In fact, the right to keep and bear arms was created by God, and merely recognized by the Constitution.

The day God armed a nation

When Israel came out of Egypt under Moses' leadership they were a nation of slaves. They were still unarmed and faced certain slaughter on the banks of the Red Sea when Pharaoh's army showed up to either destroy or enslave them once again. God intervened. God did two things at the Red Sea. First, He destroyed the most powerful standing army of that time. Second, God washed the bodies and military weapons and armor up onto the shore, for Israel to pick up and use (Exodus 14:30). We know this because shortly after that event, Israel had to fight against another nation for survival. This time they had weapons (Exodus 17:13), and God expected them to use them in battle. Israel won. Why? Because God...GOD...gave them the right to keep and bear arms.

You may respond with Scriptures that tell us to live at peace and harmony. Are they in the Bible? Absolutely, but they must be balanced out with other passages. In a time of war, you do not live at peace. When someone seeks to destroy you, you do not play nice. The wall builders in Nehemiah 4 prayed mean prayers! They prayed that their enemies would not be forgiven. They made plans to put them outside the walls, and they planned to destroy all attackers! This is just as much the heart of the Holy Bible as the peaceful verses. God is not afraid of battle and war, and Christians should adopt His mindset.

In Nehemiah's day, when Judah picked up their swords, it is not because they were looking for a fight. It is because they were looking to be left alone. A weapon at my side means that I cannot be forced; only persuaded by reason. I don't carry it because I am afraid; I carry it because it enables me to be unafraid. It does not limit the actions of those who would interact with me through reason, but it does limit the actions of those who would do so by force. It removes force from the equation. That is why carrying a gun is a civilized act.

In Joel 3:9-10 God commands Israel to beat their plowshares into swords and their pruning hooks into spears. This day is still forthcoming. In other words, the citizen farmer will be commanded to take up arms and fight for his country, because God tells him to do it. What will you do if you don't have a "sword?"

This passage of Scripture is one of the foundations for God's given right to keep and bear arms. Exodus 22:2 is the foundation for all self-defense law. "If a thief be found breaking up, and is smitten that he dies, there shall no blood be shed for him." Those are God's words. While it is true that murder, personal vengeance and intentional slaughter are all sins that merit the death penalty (Genesis 9:6), these conditions are found in the sinful heart of mankind; not in the right to keep and bear arms.

Psalm 141:1-2 tells us that it is God that teaches our hands to war and our fingers to fight. Psalm 18:34-42 talks of God's training so that His people destroy their foes in battle with military-grade weapons. Hebrews 11:32-34 commends men that subdued kingdoms in battles, and won battles against countless enemies.

In yet another forward look, the Lord reveals a coming event in Ezekiel 38 in which God calls for a sword against the invaders. In modern terms that's a firearm. To that end, Jesus even said when speaking of these days that if we did not have a "sword", we need to sell our extra garments and buy one. What would Jesus do? He would tell you to have a garage sale, and buy a Glock. It's really that practical, and God-inspired. The next time you hear the politicians weeping and gnashing their teeth over gun-toting Americans, and appealing to a perverted form of faith to justify disarmament, just think "WWJD."

These are just some of the Bible verses that provide the foundation of God's law to keep and bear arms.

God-given rights and responsibilities

Our forefathers recognized the right to keep and bear arms as a God-given right; not a government-given privilege. They also recognized the responsibility that came with the right. This is why they recognized the citizens of the nation as the militia that protected her. They did not recognize a standing army.

- The second amendment was not drafted to empower a professional State police force or military to own and carry weapons.
- The second amendment was not drafted to empower citizens to hunt.
- The second amendment was drafted to empower Joe Citizen to own and carry weapons, and have the capacity to wage war when necessary.
- The citizen is the last line of defense for this nation, and the right to keep and bear arms is integral to our national sovereignty.

Our message to you is simple; God, guts and guns made America. Keep all three.

Globalists hate your guns

The second strategy the globalists used in Nehemiah 4 was to threaten terror attacks. They intended to kill the wall builders. They never threatened to attack when the city walls were broken down and they had free access, but tyranny despises boundaries that restrict evil. Now the threats were ramping up, and now it became necessary for every citizen to keep and bear arms, both for the purposes of self-defense and for national security.

- Half the citizens guarded the walls, while the others built.
- Then they rotated the workers and the guards.
- If there was an attack, everyone picked up arms and went to battle.
- This system effectively rebuffed the globalists. It will work again.

What must we do?

It is time for every patriot to reclaim the second amendment. It is also time for America to release all liberty into the hands of we the people.

- No law or restriction of ownership of suppressors (silencers).
- No laws against magazine capacity.
- No laws against any type of firearms or armaments.
- If you want a tank, you can have one (if you can afford it).

But there's a catch.

- Every citizen has a responsibility to the national and civil defense system as well.
- Every pacifist must pay those that guard them.
- Every American must either build America, or guard it.
- Severe punishment will be doled out quickly for those who misuse their liberty.

This is the responsibility of every citizen militia, and it's found first in the Bible.

- No more pacifists.
- Every man is accountable for his use or misuse of lethal force.
- No more restrictions.
- No more playing nice with the enemy.
- Terror will be destroyed.
- America will be strong and sovereign.
- Globalism will be pushed back, and border security will be reclaimed.

YOU will play a part in doing this. Buy a gun. Learn how to use it. Practice with it. Understand the fact that it will be used to stand in defense of a nation. Your nation. Lock and load!

> *...and he that hath no sword, let him sell his garment, and buy one.* Luke 22:36

Rule #4: Keep and bear arms. Always be prepared to defend American liberty with deadly force.

Questions:

- Will you support the unrestricted right to keep and bear arms?
- Which caliber(s) of firearm will you choose to learn and use for daily protection?
- How do you need to change your approach toward globalism?
- How will you stand for the land?

Chapter 5 - Total Economic Restructure

Nehemiah 5

Several rules have emerged for America's rebuilders. They are ***all*** required steps to making America great again. Not one can be omitted or ignored.

Rule #1: Repent, and determine to become one nation under One God. Repentance is the foundation, the key ingredient to make America great again. We must get honest, we must get real, we must depart from the globalist mindset we currently love and embrace.

Rule #2: Reject globalism, reject the status quo, and identify the enemies within America. There are great enemies of American exceptionalism and liberty at work within our borders. They must be recognized as such, and must be opposed and defeated.

Rule #3: Embrace nationalism under God, and get involved. Build that wall!

Rule #4: Keep and bear arms. Prepare to defend American liberty and exceptionalism with deadly force. The people's right to keep and bear arms is necessary for the survival of a free people. There are no bad guns; only bad hearted people that may use guns. They need to be dealt with, and swiftly.

Next stop: The economy.

Edward

He goes to church regularly, and calls himself a Christian. But he spends more time with ESPN and his 401k, than his Bible. When elections come around, he always votes on one issue alone; the economy. He loves the system as it is today, because he has grown rich, increased with goods, and has need of nothing. Any talk of building a wall is met with his contempt, because he likes things just how they are. Cheap labor has padded his portfolio, and his only care is what the weekend's sports scores are. He enjoys the artificial bubble he exists in; he enjoys his slumber. Don't bother trying to awaken him.

Darrell & Marge

The bond issue for the local school board was important. The local schools lagged behind other districts in funding, and the needs were many, but Darrell & Marge couldn't afford it. Their fixed income wasn't being raised to match the cost of living, and they watched every penny. When it came to the question of schools versus food, food won out at the ballot box.

Peter

Peter had worked as a small businessman for over twenty-five years. When he started he was able to take a salary that amounted to around $15 per hour. Now, twenty-five years later, his salary was the same, but the bills were not. Peter had no pension, no retirement savings, and there were weeks when he was just happy to meet the bills. He knew things had to change somehow, someday, but for now he was just happy to put gas in the truck and food on the table.

Scott

Scott needed to declare bankruptcy and clear away the years of debt and pain. The problem was this: he couldn't afford it. He was caught between the burdens of the past and the tyranny of the present. All of the money he and his wife made went into rent, food, and transportation. They still had hopes and dreams. They were just buried under a mountain of debt.

The wall builders in Nehemiah's time nearly quit building the border wall. They had the desire, the vision, and the materials, but they could not afford to continue the work. Why? They were buried in debt. This was not debt from extravagant spending. The citizens had acquired debt to eat, to build homes, and to work their jobs. If the people were to be free, the economy had to be reformed, and swiftly.

Economic gouging

The economic problems that originated in Nehemiah's day did not originate in the global economic system. The root of the problem lay within the nation itself. The greedy were more than happy to make huge profits off of the backs of the poor, and the rank and file patriot carried a ton of debt.

Consider the economic oppression of God's people as seen by the prophet Amos:

> "Hear this, O ye that swallow up the needy, even to make the poor of the land to fail, saying, when will the new moon be gone that we may sell corn? And the sabbath, that we may set forth wheat, making the ephah small and the shekel great, and falsifying the balances by deceit? That we may buy the poor for silver, and the needy for a pair of shoes; yea, and sell

the refuse of the wheat? The Lord hath sworn by the excellency of Jacob, Surely I will never forget any of their works." Amos 8:4-7

God does not hate the wealthy, but He despises the greedy. The passage above talks about an economic system where money can be manipulated and devalued. It describes a system where the value of money is based entirely on perception, not on a solid standard that is backing it. It results in you having to pay more to buy less, and never really knowing what your buying power is. Perhaps the prophet Amos was seeing a time when the cereal box seems to shrink every year, while the costs keep going up. Perhaps he was looking ahead to a stock market economy, based entirely on perception. This passage clearly speaks of God's anger toward those who want to use cheap labor for their greed and gain. Truly, this is the foundation of much of America's immigration debate today. The rich want cheap labor and cheap wages, so they turn a blind eye to open borders and an illegal workforce.

God calls that oppression.

God also hates those that sell inferior products, things that break down and must be purchased over and over again, so that profits can go into the hands of a few, from the pockets of the poor. In Nehemiah's day, the banks and businesses that were considered "too big to fail" came under attack from the people. They were preying on the poor for their selfish gain. **This economic system will be destroyed**, because God hates it!

How bad was it?

The economic situation was so bad that there were people who had to "take" to provide for their families. They were not buying, they were just taking things as they found them. Were they stealing from the fields or stores? Or were they merely foraging and scavenging? It is not completely clear, but they were not getting by with their paychecks.

Next, there were people who were buying for their families, but they were going under in the process. They were accruing debt against their possessions to make it possible. These people literally took out second mortgages to pay for groceries.

Then there were those who had mortgaged their property just to pay their taxes. This was a Hail Mary pass to stave off debtor's prison, but it carried some adverse side effects that forced them to consider the unthinkable.

- They "sold" their land to pay taxes.
- They "sold" their kids into slavery for the balance due.
- They signed contracts that would never give them back their property.

They owed taxes every year, and had no way to make the money to pay them. They were literally losing family and property simply because of the economic policies. The greatest travesty of all is that it was made possible by their own countrymen, and the economic system that kept the people enslaved to it.

More social programs?

At this juncture, any good socialist would say that the solution is to take from the rich and give it to the poor. They would also increase the size and power of government and ramp up the entitlement programs. In their minds this would equalize the "haves" with the "have nots". After all, people are losing their homes, and mortgage backed securities are in big trouble. So big government needs to fix the economy. A socialist Nehemiah might enact TARP (Troubled Asset Relief Program) legislation to bailout the banks that are "too big to fail." Fortunately for Jerusalem and Judah, Nehemiah was not a socialist, and was not going to act on behalf of the banks. Socialism only empowers government, and enslaves people. He was going to act for the people, at the expense of the banking system. In his mind, the banks were too corrupt NOT to fail, and it was time to let some things collapse.

Most American patriots know that pandering to the banks only covers the assets of the rich, at the expense of the working man. Real solutions for Joe Citizen begin when we actually disregard the financial rules and systems that have put the people into economic bondage, or cause it to crash under its own weight. Only then can a wealth-based system be built.

In Nehemiah's day, the nobles and the rulers were the ones in power. They were the ones who could relieve the burdens of the people and enable free enterprise and the creation of wealth. Instead, they had created an economy and banking system that enslaved them.

Free enterprise is not the problem

Free enterprise was not creating the disparity between the "haves" and the "have nots." Instead, the problem was an economic system of oppression, created by the central bank. This oppressed the people. The central bank was responsible for the disappearing middle class, with its currency that could be inflated or deflated, its fluctuating interest rates, and its choke-hold on how the people were able to trade and spend in the real world.

Tear it down, and build it God's way

We don't have to reinvent the foundation of a successful economy. Once again we must look back and use what worked in the past. It is simple, but not easy, and liberty's enemies will be unhappy when the everyday American starts to prosper again.

The starting point for fixing the economy is recognizing that it must be brought down, not propped up. The commonly accepted banking practices of the day were in direct opposition to God's laws for the nation.

For example, the laws contained in the Bible show that property rights are held in high regard by God, and God's law forbids the paying of PROPERTY TAX to the government. Why? Because according to God, the government has NO LAWFUL claim to property! Yet property was being taxed, and as such it allowed government a controlling interest in something that it had no right to have. It allowed government the false "authority" to seize what did not belong to it. It is a case of government usurpation and economic oppression, made possible by policies that deviated from God's banking laws. People today are silly enough to believe that all God cares about is organ music, potlucks, and church committees, when Scripture makes it plain that He is very interested in matters like economics.

The question could be asked; how do we fund government, if property taxes are an illegal tax in the courts of heaven? God DID allow for taxes to be levied against profits made, but profits were the only thing that was taxed. And they were taxed at a flat rate. 1 Samuel 8:15.

That rate? **10%.**

That tax was also something to be *voluntarily* paid by the people. There was no department of revenue, no IRS, no audits, no tax police. If the people did not do it willingly, God judged them for it. That was in HIS hands, NOT THE GOVERNMENT'S hands! God designed it that way to keep the government from becoming oppressive. As soon as government has power to tax and enslave, it does not take long for it to believe that it is God.

At the heart of this discussion is the role of government from a Biblical perspective. If Judah was going to be one nation under God, shouldn't they find out and implement what God has to say about the affairs of State? Frankly, if America is one nation

UNDER God, shouldn't Biblical perspectives matter just as much today?

If Nehemiah was going to make his nation great again, he would be forced to deal with excessive taxation and monetary policies from God's point of view. Government and monetary policies exist for one reason...to secure the liberties of the people under God. Government serves the people...not vice-versa.

It's incumbent on the church to engage government...or government will forget there is a God...and it will not take long before it begins to think that IT is God. History has nothing good to say about nations when that happens. Apparently even God is interested in limited government and the powers that it can exercise.

Socialists would say that Nehemiah-like reforms tie government's hands and won't let it operate effectively. Admittedly, Nehemiah moved to tie its hands to rectify its overreach. Sometimes you have to slap the hand that is in the cookie jar. This chapter records some of his government cut-backs. He truly did run a lean, mean, governing machine.

The end-result of such an economic move is that it creates a form of capitalism that forces the government to operate efficiently. God established the tax cap for government, and He expects it to operate within the 10% figure that He gives to it for its overhead. It must prioritize if it cannot raise the tax ceiling, and pass along its waste to the Citizen.

When government cannot TAKE more, the only recourse it has for increasing its revenue, is to enable the PEOPLE to MAKE more. Right government always frees people to prosper, and it realigns the burdens to the proper shoulders. Contrast that with the socialist position we mentioned in the previous chapter which says that government can tax 100%, and then be a Nanny State.

That position is contrary to the law of God.

If we are serious about being one nation under God, we must reject the socialist Kool-Aid, socialist politics, and socialist wannabes, regardless of their party affiliation. They must be labeled for what they truly are; anti-Christ.

What about usury, or charging interest?

More specifically, the practice of making money on money... usury or interest...was unlawful according to God. The banks could charge usury to foreign nations, but not to citizens of its own people. The law permitted them to make money by investing, and selling goods and services, but not by loaning out money to citizens. It makes sense when we remember that the love of money is the root of all evil, and that completely neuters any notion of a central bank.

According to the Bible, money...whatever it may have been... was merely intended to be a means of exchange. NOTHING LESS...NOTHING MORE. As soon as you legalize the concept of selling money, it's not long before class warfare is the result, and the rich begin ruling over the poor. The injustices that stem from that create a situation utterly abhorrent to God!

Abolish the Fed

Where does that put the Federal Reserve and the multitude of politicians that support it? In the crosshairs! Any financial system consisting of smoke and mirrors, and based merely on perceived value is destined to complete collapse. Look no further than the debt figures presented earlier in this book. It is unsustainable, and the current prosperity is a complete illusion.

Doing what is right doesn't require consultation with bankers...with the Congress or Senate...with the lobbyists...or even with the global community that profits off the backs of those blessed by God. Listen to the charge Nehemiah brings against the "bankers"...the financiers...the economic system in general.

> Nehemiah 5:8 - *And I said unto them, We after our ability have redeemed our brethren the Jews, which were sold unto the heathen; and will ye even sell your brethren? or shall they be sold unto us? Then held they their peace, and found nothing to answer.*

In a nutshell, he reminded them of his efforts to redeem the nation, and indicted them for unlawful financial practices that were destroying the nation. They may have been legal, but they were not lawful. One thing is certain; God did not deify the banking practices of that day, nor does He today. There are no banks and economic practices that are "too big to fail."

The future success or failure of the American economic system will not be based on its size, reach, influence, assets, or opinion of the global community. It will be based SOLELY on compliance with the laws of God.

WWND

America needs to ask the question, "What would Nehemiah do?" It worked effectively then, and made Israel wealthy again. It will work for America today. The answer? Total economic reform, based on the Bible.

- No property tax.
- Forgiveness of loans and debts enacted before the wall-building time.
- No government interests in land holdings.
- Complete restoration of family lands and trusts.
- Zero percent interest for citizens.

- Fixed currencies that cannot be inflated or deflated to manipulate the people.
- A government tax cap of 10 percent.

It worked then. It will work now. Which side are you on?

A false balance is abomination to the Lord: but a just weight is his delight. Proverbs 11:1

Rule #5: Abandon the global economy and its commonly accepted practices. Return to a wealth-based, biblically founded national economy.

Questions:

- Are you profiting or losing based on today's economic system?
- Would you agree with Nehemiah's reforms, or oppose them?
- Since God said the corrupt global economic system will collapse, how can you prepare accordingly?

Chapter 6 - Never Negotiate with Globalists

Nehemiah 6

Brian

He was a well-spoken presenter with excellent credentials. Brian donated time to charitable service, attended church services, and had been married to the same woman for twenty-five years. He and his wife had done missions outreaches in Uganda besides. As a candidate he was solidly-supported in his run for city council in a conservative area, because he was also a Republican. However, he also condoned the building of the local mosque, sat on the board of a refugee center that was primarily islamic in nature, and took his last vacation to Cuba. Those who spoke against his social views were summarily dismissed, and he was handily elected into office. What's wrong with America? We are not only facing enemies without; we are electing them within.

Charley

Charley was a solid State legislator with a nice family. He was supported by a regional gun organization, and met with the local tea party, gaining their support. When he decided to run for the position of Representative to Washington, D.C., many conservatives supported him, campaigned and voted for him. Shortly after his election Charley voted to raise the debt ceiling, and then repeated the action time and time again. He also ignored those that put him into office in the first place, moving and staffing consistently to the left. Today he is a U.S. Senator that wields great power. He is also a pseudo-conservative and a part of the D.C. problem; not the solution.

Simon

As a businessman Simon traveled in and out of Washington, D.C. on a regular basis. While there he had the opportunity to meet with Congressmen and women on a repeated basis. Some sought Simon out for discussion, and he had their personal cell phone numbers. But when Simon stopped contributing to their campaigns, everything seemed to change with most of them. They still knew who he was, but the relationships weren't the same. When Simon offered one Congressman a flash drive with information regarding immigration and refugee issues in Northern Colorado, it was flatly refused. Rejected. It wasn't information they wanted, nor did he have the money they craved to retain power in Congress.

Once again, each story is true. They are drawn from the experiences of many years, and behind every one of them is a real person (or people). Some are a part of the problem; others are part of the solution. Where do you stand?

Nehemiah was having success building the wall, in chapter 6. He had faced opposition, apathy, terror attacks, and economic woes that stood in his way. He was determined to restore his nation to the status that it enjoyed in previous generations, and his efforts were paying off. BUT, the enemy within were angry, and they had not gone away. As the walls started to grow, the enemies outside of Judah could not simply overpower Nehemiah and the wall builders. Their opposition had to be cloaked in political spin, their tactics had to change. Much like we see in America today.

The enemy was well-entrenched in the system of Jerusalem in Nehemiah's day. The unknown lurked outside the walls, but it had been assisted by the enemy within. Now that they were losing, they employed all of their options. Many of these are used today. We will discuss them, and more. So what are the tactics of the enemy?

Enemy Tactic 1: Reach Across The Aisle

You have heard it before, and it always comes from the losers *to* the winners. The winners are told to "reach across the aisle." In most cases, when that term is used, the compromise associated with it is actually lauded as a quality in a politician.

Not so in Nehemiah's day, and not so today. When the globalists saw that Nehemiah was surprisingly effective in his grassroots efforts, they resorted to "negotiating." Five times they instructed Nehemiah to "reach across the aisle," and in each case it only would have weakened Nehemiah's efforts. Rest assured, when this tactic is deployed, it is only designed to weaken the patriots who have undertaken the work. It adds nothing to you, and takes your effectiveness from you. Nehemiah did not cave in, and neither should you. When they were unsuccessful, they resorted to branding Nehemiah with unsavory titles. He wasn't playing by their game, and they quickly resorted to ridicule and ad-hominem as their weapons of choice.

Many politicians (in both major parties) want to perpetuate the current system, so this is not just dangerous. It is treasonous. Do not reach across the aisle, and ask yourself this clarifying question; How do they benefit if I believe what they're saying, or comply with them?

Enemy Tactic 2: Be Offended

The underlying premise behind every one of the enemy tactics came down to this: "We are offended." In truth, they were likely jealous of Nehemiah's resolve and success, but the enemy within can't just come out of the closet and say that. They cannot tolerate national exceptionalism, or those who promote it. Their jealousy needs to be cloaked in some form of legitimacy, and being offended is the best way to gain the sympathy of the weak, underachievers, and the global community. Birds of a feather, flock together.

Recognize offended-ness for what it really is! Be it an angry teenager, #BlackLivesMatter, the "politically correct", or ANTIFA, offended-ness is a sign of two things; a weak position, and a lack of power. They would overpower you and crush you if they could, but they cannot. This is why they resort to being offended. It is designed to weaken your resolve.

Being offended doesn't make you right; it just makes you offended!

Being offended is how losers dictate the terms of surrender to the winners!

Winners need to read those last two sentences again.

It is time for America's prevailing culture to stop waving the white flag of surrender, and re-assert their dominance again. For that to occur, rebuilders need to recognize offended-ness for what it is. It is merely an attempt to manipulate God-fearing patriots into silence, and acquiesce to tyrants or underachieving cultures. Never surrender. Do not slow down when those attacks come. The mere existence of offended losers is an indication that the rebuilders are winning.

The rule for rebuilders? Double down. It will upset the enemy within, but hopefully by now you have realized you will never convert them anyway. They will never be won over, they are not to be negotiated with.

They are to be defeated.

John said it best in Revelation 22:11 - *He that is unjust, let him be unjust still: and he which is filthy, let him be filthy still: and he that is righteous, let him be righteous still: and he that is holy, let him be holy still.*

Do not compromise with that which is destined to defeat.

Why slow down, and why cower because of their manipulation attempts? In the book of Acts, there were riots, uproars, and Christ's disciples were accused of "turning the world upside down." Coming from the corrupt establishment, that is actually a compliment. Why did it happen? Because they refused to let the establishment's offended-ness dictate their course of action. If it happened then, why should it be any different today?

Enemy Tactic 3: Isolate Your Faith

More often than not, patriots and conservatives are expected to leave their convictions behind if they are "lucky" enough to gain a seat of power. In Nehemiah's day, he was "encouraged" to hide within the temple, and keep his convictions inside its four walls. It was presented by the globalists as his safe space, with the inference that carrying his faith outside of the four walls would be dangerous to himself and society. In truth, taking his faith outside of the four walls WAS dangerous...to globalism. It promoted national exceptionalism; which is precisely why the established ruling class did not want him to do it.

What did Nehemiah do? He rejected that thinking, and kept building the wall. He kept his faith in God, wore it proudly, because he KNEW what the nation should be. Nehemiah actually used his faith to build his nation. We need to do the same thing.

Enemy Tactic 4: Criminalize the Patriots

When all else fails, and globalists are at their wits end, they will seek to criminalize rebuilders.

Tyranny never begins at the muzzle of a gun. It begins in think tanks and legislative halls. Once a legal foundation is in place, it ends at the muzzle of a gun. Their gun. When Nehemiah continued to build and prosper they levied accusations of treason and sedition. When Daniel prayed to God in his day, tyrants passed legislation to make him a criminal. This took him to the lion's den and back again. When the three Hebrew children exercised freedom of worship, tyrants conferred legal guilt upon them. It took them into the fiery furnace, and back again.

Today, when bakers refuse to bake wedding cakes for homosexual "marriage", legislation is crafted to make them into criminals. One would expect to hear of that in Russia in the 1930s, but not in America in the 21st century. Then again, when you understand that legislation designed to criminalize freedom-loving people is a tyrant's weapon, it is not so far-fetched. It is expected, and rebuilders need to know it is coming.

Rebuild anyway.

Whether you know it or not, you are probably a "criminal" right now. Laws have been, and are being passed, to make you into one. Even though they may not be enforced at the moment, they are in place and on the books, ready for tyrannical use. One study says the average American commits three (or more) felonies per *day*, though they don't even know it. No, that figure is not a typo. Today, there are thousands of federal crimes, and the number is constantly increasing. It brings to mind the words of the Roman historian Tacitus: "The more corrupt the State, the more numerous the laws."

You. Are. Here.

What is the rule for rebuilders? Double down. Rebuilding America is not right because it is popular with globalists. Never subject your efforts to their approval. When the attacks come, take ownership of the narrative, reframe the fight, defy tyranny, and keep building anyway. If they insist on being offended, be offensive. The best defense is a good offense, so go on the attack. Often times you will have to redefine the premise they attack with, but it is imperative to recognize what they are up to. Refuse to be intimidated into quitting, reject them publicly, expose their fallacies publicly, and continue to rebuild. And if you are not a "criminal" yet, you may want to ask yourself when you will become one. Not by virtue of you breaking the law, but by virtue of them framing law to criminalize your liberty. Everyone will be made to care, and you should define your red lines before the stakes are too high. You will both acquiesce and come under their thumb, or you will thumb your nose at their intimidation, and make a stand. Rebuilding requires strength of character, and taking a stand.

Pushing back against globalists and seasoned governmental politicians and bureaucrats is hard work. They know it; they have made it that way. They have stacked to deck to pressure you into compromise. Globalists believe they can paralyze you, and keep you beholden to their agenda. Since you must engage them, **you must understand how America's present government works.**

"Therefore I run, but not uncertainly; I fight, but not as one that beats the air." 1 Corinthians 9:26

"Be wise as serpents and harmless as doves." Matthew 10:16

"Lest satan should get an advantage of us, for we are not ignorant of his devices." 2 Corinthians 2:11

What is politics, anyway?

Politics is simply the adjudication of power. It is who rules whom. Some nations conduct politics at the end of a gun barrel. They kill people, steal property, rape women, and rule tyrannically. Other nations rule through laws. These laws only work when the government is willing to fairly and impartially enforce them. When too many laws and regulations are written, this becomes impossible. Selective enforcement and special interests then manipulate the government, and the people become enslaved.

There is an old quote sometimes attributed to George Washington about government and politics. *"Government is not reason; it is not eloquent. It is force. Like fire, it is a dangerous servant and a fearful master. Never for a moment should it be left to irresponsible action."*

In chapter 3, we shared on the need for you to be involved with rebuilding the wall. You will have to become involved with government and politics. If you want to sit on the sidelines, you are a part of the problem; not the solution. The enemy can manipulate you, and use your silence as consent for their globalist agenda. But you are not getting involved to get along. You are getting involved to upset the status quo.

Nehemiah operated from a position of strength. In the United States, "we the people" have the power, but government and globalism don't want us to know how powerful we are! In this chapter we will reveal some of the tactics the enemy does not want you to know, or to use.

You must engage the globalists, and even the party pukes (both main political parties have them) in government. They will want you to play by their rules. DO NOT COMPLY! Their rules are designed to keep them in power, put rebuilders at a disadvantage, and discourage you from challenging their grip. They want your money, your vote, and your capitulation. If they can make rebuilders compromise, they win. What would have happened if the globalists would have convinced Nehemiah to pause and negotiate? Today, there would be no wall. But we can win, if we understand how the globalists and entrenched politicians operate. The establishment knows that, and it terrifies them.

YOU are the most powerful force in American government. You! Yes, you! If you understand how things work in our present political environment, you can shape government at every level of society. This is why you must be snake smart about how things work! You must use these tactics against the enemy, instead of merely grumbling and letting them control you. It all begins with you understanding your power. YOUR power. If you will oppose the enemy, he will flee at some point in time. It may take a while, but your relentless pressure and understanding of how things work will pay off. Nehemiah knew his authority. It's time that you know yours.

Are you ready to learn, and fight back? Here are some things they don't want you to know.

Your role in government

There are two ways to interact with government.

The first option is to run for political office and serve within government. Most people will not, or cannot do this. We pride ourselves on being a government of the people, but most of the people want to ignore this option. Or they legitimately do not have the time, talent, or resources. But if you want better leaders, maybe one of them needs to be you! Maybe you need to step up and sacrifice. After all, we all agree that there must be people of integrity in government to cast the votes, rule from the bench, and operate the affairs of State. Why not you?

The second option is less direct, yet very good at affecting a desired political outcome. Enter the citizen advocate. There was only one Nehemiah, yet there were thousands working behind the scenes. Each of these rebuilders were just as important as Nehemiah. He would not have restored the nation without them. They had to help him build, hold him accountable, hold the enemy accountable, push the agenda forward that he carried, and push back against global influences in their neighborhood. They served as citizen advocates for nationalism that helped move the political box from outside of the system.

With the right tactics, and an uncompromising attitude, rebuilders can make government fear the forces coming against it from the outside. We can influence and push those inside government to do what is right. We can move the political box, whether they like it or not. We can tell government what is right, and then use force to make them do the right thing. At the very least, your role in government is this. You cannot do this by just ranting on facebook, or sending emails. You cannot stand by merely talking to your circle of friends. You must exert political pressure and pain where power is in place, and that will move the political box.

The ONLY reason the globalists did not attack Nehemiah and bury him alive is because they were scared of him, and the support base he had assembled. It really is that simple. They tried intimidation to get Nehemiah to self-destruct, but Nehemiah was too smart for that. He could see the globalists were afraid of him and his agenda, which is right where he wanted them. If you are winning, why negotiate a truce (your surrender) with them?

For too long, patriots, Christians, and the founding culture of America have played too nice to be feared. This is why the politicians no longer listen to many of us. Pain is the only thing that will back them down, and move the political box.

With a right understanding of the political machine, average patriots can work as advocates for the rebuilding effort, and inflict pressure and pain where it is needed to back down thugs. From this point we are going to assume that you are involved, or willing to be involved in wall-building, and need to know some of the issues you will face (and how to deal with them).

The political box

Many think that proper education will move the box, and produce better government. People think that if we can tell people in government about the "right" thing, they will automatically "see the light," and do what we say. So, how's that working for you? It is obvious it has not worked. Why? Do you think that educating the system on truth, justice, fairness, and equity will motivate it when it prefers to keep people weak, and itself strong? You have not hurt the corrupt political machine in any way, so it has no reason to change.

There are two primary reasons why this does not work. First, education takes a long time. Even in a best case scenario, when leaders are good and want to learn, it takes a long time for education efforts to have a positive effect. We are reaping the fruit of the hippie generation, nearly 50 years later. They went into the schools and universities of the land, and indoctrinated thousands of students. Only now is the fruit coming to harvest. If you want to use education, plan to invest your entire life sowing into people's hearts with little-to-no-return. It takes a long time. If you choose to work as an educator, be prepared for frustration, hindrance by the machine in place, and a lifetime of work with little fruit. You must also be prepared to find like-minded people within that circle, and be prepared to work as a coalition to stand against globalism and evil. This is the only way you will wield power in this realm.

Second, government usually does not seek enlightenment. It seeks total control. The prophet Samuel warned Israel in 1 Samuel 8 of the tyranny that kingly dictators would bring. The story is still the same today. The final check against tyranny is power in your hands. This was the principle of the Constitution and the Bill of Rights. They were designed to restrict government; not you. Combatting attacking politics will require more than merely educating others. You must wield power enough to inflict pain on the political machine. That is the only thing that will move the political box. How does the box work?

Government and politics live inside a defined realm; a box. This is where government happens. Legislation is made and signed, and people come in and out to present their issues, wants and needs. Inside the box there are people like council members, congressmen and women, presidents, and governors. Also inside this box are government employees, aides, and the staffs that support each of these people. There is another entrenched group inside the box that we hear about all the time. They are lobbyists, special interest groups, and other assisting groups that know how government operates. They represent good or evil. They can represent a second amendment group, right to life, homosexual issues, or global trade. All of these people are inside the box.

Outside the box are forces that move the box. Some of these are quite powerful, or at least they want to be. Studies, articles, news reports and "social buzz" are all powerful things to a government. All of these things are used to move the box; to push it closer to the outcome that a certain group desires. If a noisy minority starts to scream about an issue, and the news media picks up on their voices, government pays attention...IF...the negative media is going to cost them money and votes. Losing both is a source of pain to the powerful. Cost them money and votes, and the box moves your way. Cost them nothing, and the box moves where they want it to go. Get the picture?

The Bible often shows the prophet filling this role throughout the Old Testament. Prophets had a unique way of creating pain for tyrannical kings who deserved it, and their efforts moved the box. When Elijah told Ahab to gather the people to Mount

Carmel, and it would rain, Ahab did exactly as Elijah instructed. That's because Elijah had created pain for the king, enough to make him listen. The church seeks to evangelize the political machine, and this is why it is ineffective at forcing change in government. It will not be won over, so be the prophet.

Today the media frequently ignores the voices they despise, and chooses the voices that suit their agenda. They are often propagandists, and depending on the administration, they may actually live inside the box themselves! So you must figure out ways to make the box people suffer, and then it will move your way.

Today's true journalists usually live in the alternative media. Don't count on any revolutionaries to come up in the ranks of the mainstream media. You may know of a website, blogger or writer that is frequently disdained by the mainstream press. They may be closer to the truth than the propagandists want you to know, so they are demonized by those inside the box! Pay attention! You may want to work with some of those people, so that you can become part of a powerful force outside the box. When you cannot become ignored, you must be addressed. You need to become the builders of government, and also the destroyers of evil legislation, agendas, and globalist thought. You must learn how to move that political box. You must learn how to create pain for a corrupt political regime.

Lobbyists will do your hard work...for pay. They live inside the box. They know who to pay off. They know who will vote in certain ways. However, *the most powerful voice to government is yours*. When you demand a response, and they respond, you have power. When you band together with like-minded rebuilders, and work to cost globalists votes and money, you become a political powerhouse; a force that has great potential to move the box!

I know somebody in government

Some readers may know someone in political office. Big deal. People in power have been using their status to dupe people for centuries. There are many gullible people that think that they have a certain degree of power or influence, just because they shook someone's hand, had their picture taken, or have chats with a governmental official from time to time. Congratulations. If they ignore you, you have just been betrayed. Are they afraid of you?

There is a huge difference between power and access. A Congressman can take your call, send you a letter addressing you by name, or even listen. They may even appoint you to a committee, or give you their cell phone number. **But if you don't change their vote, you have absolutely no political power.** You merely have access, and most people settle for this. They would rather think they are helping than do the confrontive, difficult, disciplinary work of holding government in check. If this is you, you must reset your thinking and your approach. You are not an asset at this point; you are a liability to liberty. You must be willing to be a pain in the neck.

You must have power with governmental leaders; not access. Power will get you access, but access will never get you power. You need to tell a politician that he or she will vote your way, or they will feel pain. If you want to change a nation, it is better to be feared by government, than liked by government. In many regards, this is where citizens have failed. Today, free Americans fear the government, but it should be the other way around. The government should fear the people, and we are playing too nice.

Let's go back to the basic premise for a moment. You are the most powerful part of government. You pay the taxes. You vote. You are paying attention. You want your issues to be addressed. The globalist will tell you that you are an idealist, passionate, and that the world doesn't work that way. Disregard them! Then find a way to make them hurt. Like Nehemiah, you must work hard to build the wall, and that means you will have to exercise your power so that government pays attention...to you. And when they are running scared because of you, never compromise or surrender.

The hypocrisy of many activists today

Whether you are inside government, or outside working to address some of the issues we face, do not over-commit yourself to entrenched activists until you know them personally. Just because someone has a label (e.g., gun rights supporter, pro-life, conservative, etc.), doesn't mean they are truly what they represent. Many activists today will sell out power for access. It gives them cushy jobs. Consider some of the right-to-life directors that complain about abortion. Behind the scenes they refuse to ally with others that stand for life. Sometimes, they make a good living by serving in pregnancy centers. What happens if abortion is found to be illegal? What will happen to their funding, their center, and their base of power? Their money? Many activists are hypocrites that are making a good living *fighting* problems instead of banding together to *solve* them. Don't always assume that activists involved in good causes actually seek our restoration as a nation. Some of them profit handsomely from decrying the evils in society, and if those evils are resolved, they are out of work.

You may think this has drifted far from the book of Nehemiah, but the reverse is true. Nehemiah had to know the tactics of the globalists in his day. Nehemiah's enemies would have LOVED it if he would have started fighting them, and put the solution on hold. He had to know their strategies, and have his own strategies to defeat them. You must do the same.

But if you want to move the box, the odds are stacked against you, right? ***Wrong***. Once again, you need to understand how government and politics work. Consider this example. The homosexual community is about four percent of the national population, yet they win political victories at every level. Are they a majority element in society? No. Are they morally or spiritually right? Absolutely not. How then, do they win their political battles? Because they understand the rules of the game, and are counting on your ignorance. Or they're counting on intimidation tactics to keep you out of the game. They are willing to be bold, be disliked, run to government (instead of avoiding it), and fight until they win. They know how to inflict the pain needed to move the box. Are you willing to do the same? If you are, read on; there's something else you must understand.

How many does it take?

How many does it take to win an election? The obvious answer would be 50 percent of the population plus 1. A simple majority of the population. Actually, this is false, because there are various factors that narrow this field. For instance, in any district, there will be those that cannot vote (felons, illegals, children, aliens, etc.). Generally, only 70 percent of any given district can vote. That being the case, all you need now to win is 35 percent plus 1. Election won, right? Wrong. We must narrow the field even more. For instance, not everyone is registered to vote! Many times only 50 percent of a district is actually registered! The winning number is now down to 25 percent plus 1, for a district victory. But that figure only holds true if each of these voters show up at the polls, or properly fill out and mail in their ballots! That rarely happens, so the field narrows even more!

Consider this valuable piece of information. In presidential elections usually only 30 percent of the people turn out to vote!

State and local elections have voter turnout that ranges from 20 to 5 percent! At this juncture, if there are no other variables, elections are often winnable with only 15 percent plus 1 of the voting bloc. But wait! There's more!

In the middle of this mix we find the hard-core voters begin to emerge. Frequently 10 percent will vote for team R, no matter what. Another 10 percent will vote for team D regardless. The third parties will support their candidates with another 3-4 percent of the vote. When everything has been narrowed down, this leaves 6-8 percent of any city, county, or district as a voting population that can be moved or swayed. They are "in play," and that is who you must target to win an election.

You can win elections and score victories for America by moving only 3-4 percent of your local population to vote for your candidate, cause or proposal! On top of that, if you are causing the other side pain (eg, costing them votes and/or money), you are a political powerhouse. And your name may not even be on the ballot.

These are the rules we need to apply, to win the victories that the others have won for years! It's estimated that only 5 percent of the total population were involved in the Revolutionary War. Today, we can turn policy with only 4 percent plus 1. In one local election last year, a city council race was decided by four votes! Four votes! When you are involved, you make the difference. You can find four votes, and change the outcome of government. You can stop the globalist advance! Never compromise!

Politicians will not like you

If you know the tactics, and use them against the establishment, politicians will not like you. You must settle this before you get into the fight. You have the potential to cause them pain. Today, many politicians don't want to do what voters dislike.

Many times they like to do nothing! The status quo is one of the greatest forces in politics today. It is up to you to change that. By now it should be at the forefront of your mind; you may have to create trouble and cause pain.

Politicians do not like angry voters, public embarrassment, no money, lack of good press, and loss of support. When you're creating this environment for them, you are being successful. If they do not agree with your position on an issue, they will use several tactics against you.

Here is a sampling of tactics that politicians have used on us during the last decade. They are all attempts to manipulate us into silence. All because we were making them hurt.

- First, they will try to ignore you, so you will go away.
- If you don't go away, they may try to schmooze you, and make you a friend (and still ignore your issue).
- If you still don't go away, they may threaten you, your business, and your reputation.

Keep building the wall.

When politicians behave this way, you are on target. Do not negotiate your surrender, but instead, double down! Nehemiah faced threats, but he kept building anyway. He was right; they were wrong! Double down!

If you still will not go away, Politicians will try to "educate" you. You may hear them tell you:

- "We don't do things that way."
- "I really can't do anything about that."
- "You are hurting the party."
- "You don't understand."
- "We need to be reasonable, not radical."
- "We need to educate others first."

- "We need to get in the majority (as a party) before we can consider that."
- "Maybe we can fix it next year."
- "Half a loaf is better than none."
- "If we did what you want, we would end up with something worse."
- "But we will lose."

Finally, a politician may try to buy you off. How?

- They may offer to attend an event, church service, community meeting, etc.
- They may offer you a position on a committee or council.
- They may suggest that you act as an advisor to them regularly.
- They may ask you to work for them on their campaign.

Remember this. The only thing that matters about a politician is how they vote!

One question you must ask.

When you hear anyone connected with politics speak, ask yourself this very important question.

"How does the politician (group, party) benefit if I believe them?"

Rest assured, if their lips are moving, they want you to believe something that is benefiting someone important to them. Believe it or not, every one of these issues come into play in Nehemiah 6, and it's critical that you understand these elements of wall building.

When to fight.

How do we know when to engage government in a battle? After all, aren't we supposed to live at peace with everyone, including government? Absolutely. Or as the Apostle Paul says in Romans 12, as much as possible. There is still a time for war if it becomes necessary. With America in the shape that it's in today, now is not a time for surrender to a corrupt system.

Many years ago a group of political consultants developed a four-question framework that rated each question on a scale of 1 to 10. Its name? Red Fox Four. When you try to evaluate whether to move forward or stand back with an issue or cause, these four questions will help you clarify whether it is worth making the fight.

1. Win or lose, just by making the fight, do you add people or money to your cause?
2. Win or lose, just by making the fight, do you help your friends and allies?
3. Win or lose, just by making the fight, do you hurt your enemies and their allies?
4. Win *and* lose, just by making the fight, what is the value of the fight?

Never give up

If you are reading this closing paragraph, chances are you care deeply about America. You may well be involved already, but have not been as effective as you want. Nehemiah knew his enemy. He also know how the system operated in his day. These tools are strategies that you must now put to work. Pick your battles. Know your enemy. Double down on your fight. Attend the meetings. Rebut the enemy. Create pain for the enemy. Do whatever it takes. You are a force to be reckoned with in government. Let them know that you will not go away until your cause, God's cause, is dealt with.

The fourth verse of our national anthem, "The Star Spangled Banner," closes with these words.

Then conquer we must, when our cause it is just,
And this be our motto, "In God is our trust."
And long may the star-spangled banner yet wave,
O'er the land of the free, and the home of the brave.

> *And from the days of John the baptist until now the kingdom of heaven suffereth violence, and the violent take it by force.* Matthew 11:12 (Jesus, 30 A.D.)

Rule #6: Refuse to be intimidated, take the initiative and go on the offense.

Questions:

- What do you need to do, in order to apply what you have learned about government?
- What are your principles; those issues in life that are no-compromise. What will you do, to demand government makes just and right laws in this area?
- Do you fear government, or intend to make government fear and respect you? You can't have it both ways.

Chapter 7 - Tighten the Screws

Nehemiah 7

There is a long list of people found in chapter 7 that had returned to Jerusalem. Nehemiah was working to better their world, but he only selected a few to lead them. This was the picture of small and limited government. They had to carry the vision he carried, and not their own agenda. Nehemiah's leaders had to embrace the rules he had established!

Rule 1:   **Rule #1:**   Repent, and determine to become one nation under One God. Repentance is the foundation, the key ingredient to make America great again. We must get honest, we must get real, we must depart from the globalist mindset we currently love and embrace.

Rule 2:   **Rule #2:**   Reject globalism, reject the status quo, and identify the enemies within America. There are great enemies of American exceptionalism and liberty at work within our borders. They must be recognized as such, and must be opposed and defeated.

Rule 3:   **Rule #3:**   Embrace nationalism under God, and get involved. Build that wall!

Rule 4:   **Rule #4:**   Keep and bear arms. Prepare to defend American liberty and exceptionalism with deadly force. The people's right to keep and bear arms is necessary for the survival of a free people. There are no bad guns;

only bad hearted people that may use guns. They need to be dealt with, and swiftly.

Rule 5:   **Rule #5:**   Abandon the global economy and its commonly accepted practices. Return to a wealth-based, biblically founded national economy.

Rule 6:   **Rule #6:**   Refuse to be intimidated, take the initiative and go on the offense. Government must be of the people, by the people and for the people.

There is a problem with many conservatives, Christians and patriots today. They don't trust anyone except themselves. Are you one? The reasons are well-founded for many, because they have been burned. Liberals, globalist ministers, politicians, ex-spouses, even pastors have been complicit in betraying the hopes and dreams of many American patriots. Many have quit the fight for selfish interest. Others have stopped because it's hard. Some patriots have tried to join with others, as long as they could lead. None of these approaches will save America. Nehemiah could not rebuild the nation alone and we can't do the job by ourselves either. He had to have their trust, and they had to have his. Nehemiah commissioned Hanani to leave the comforts of his former position and serve in the affairs of state. He was chosen as the national secretary of defense! Nehemiah lists Hanani's qualifications as a faithful man who feared God above many. He was a man who could be trusted to tighten the screws, and implement God's rules in the rebuilding effort.

Abandonment theology

Roles in government have been abandoned by many Christians for various reasons. First, many Christians have been told they will be raptured off of the planet and don't need to worry about what happens. After all, God will take care of it, and what happens on earth is of little importance. They could not be more wrong.

Isaiah 9:6 tells us that the government shall be upon Christ's shoulder, but He intends to delegate that authority...to you!

- 2 Timothy 2:12 speaks of Christians reigning with Christ. So does Revelation 20:6.
- 1 Corinthians 6:3 tells us that Christians will judge angels in the age to come.
- Matthew 19:28 says that the twelve apostles will sit upon thrones, judging the twelve tribes of Israel!

Where does the training for governmental authority in the age to come begin? It begins with you. It begins now! In the early days of the American colonies, government was very important to the colonists. Today, it ranks somewhere between football and a colonoscopy. It's time to turn that around.

> *When the righteous are in authority, the people rejoice: but when the wicked beareth rule, the people mourn.* Proverbs 29:2

Hanani became the gatekeeper of the city under the appointment of Nehemiah. Without gates, walls only serve to redirect the flow of traffic. Gates, times of entry and exit, and those that may enter (and those that cannot) are critical issues pertaining to border security. The wall is one thing, but there must be a foundation for policies that determine who comes, who goes, who stays, who leaves. More importantly, the leaders that control these issues are particularly critical. After all, politics is the adjudication of power; it is who rules whom. The oversight of these things must be put into trusted hands. America needs gatekeepers at every level!

Hanani wasn't the only one that was appointed. Nehemiah also appointed watchers for the walls from the inhabitants of Jerusalem. There was not a standing army; there was a citizen militia. Everybody contributed to the cause. There is no record of a police force. Everyone was armed, and every citizen was now called to patrol and guard the city walls, protecting from invasion. This was a part of the duty of being a citizen. If you didn't like it, you were welcome to live outside the walls.

The list

With Hanani in charge, Nehemiah began to take account of those that lived inside the walls. With the help of the local officials he found the birth records. Everyone would be identified for citizenship based on their birth certificates. Now was the time to account for your heritage. Most of Israel guarded their birth records with fervor, and could account for their heritage. Some could not, or would not reveal their identities. In Nehemiah's time, anyone who would have paid $3.2 million to conceal their college records or birth information, would have been deemed ineligible to serve in government. In America, they may be elected President. Liberals call that "progress," but it's a sure sign that the nation has been compromised by foreign interests.

Coming as no surprise, some of the resident aliens in Nehemiah's day were employed in leadership roles where it was illegal for them to serve. People administering the rule of law included those that could not reveal their birth records. Nehemiah was not comfortable outsourcing the leadership roles of government into the hands of these people. Their heritage was too connected to globalism. Their spiritual roots were corrupted by idolatry. Their economic framework was debt-based; not wealth-based. Their loyalties did not lie with his nation. They could be corrupted by enemies from other lands. They would not rule the land!

Removing the foreigners from government guaranteed openings for the natural-born citizens who qualified; the Levites. It also required them to purify their lives and step up to the task.

The cause of rebuilding the land was serious business, and they had to step into government; not out of it. They had to become the judges, administrators, clerks and planners. Every position of leadership was reserved for the natural born citizen. From the priesthood to national security and defense, no muslim, atheist, or outsider would be allowed to lead again. Only those loyal to the land would lead, and every one had to answer one basic question to be considered: *"Where's the birth certificate?"*

Let's talk outsourcing

Here's the bottom line; outsourcing the American dream is stupid. The United States of America has outsourced everything, from our national defense, to our faith and our values. At one point we even outsourced the presidency! We have placed our wellbeing into the hands of people who have no allegiance to American sovereignty.

In the 1930's America suffered through a great economic depression, but it was overcome. How? The American industrial and manufacturing system was in place. We produced, farmed and worked our way back into a place of stability. Today we have closed our factories, our family farms are disappearing, and most Americans exist only as consumers. Very dependent consumers. They produce nothing, yet expect everything. And while the dollar holds, the world is happy to manufacture it for us. But what happens once our dollar is found to be worthless? What happens when the global community turns against America, and wants to finally bring us to our knees? Nothing good, if everything is made overseas.

It is time to bring everything back home again. Food production, energy, manufacturing, everything should be reconsidered and reordered. In order for this to happen, America is going to need some gates, and the ability to regulate what flows in and out through them.

Controlling the gates

Once Nehemiah had built the walls and had secured the majority of the nation, he had to address the gates of the city. We must do the same in America, by reclaiming our national production. Consider for a moment that "American-made" vehicle that is purchased and driven in America. It may have been assembled in the USA, but it wasn't produced here! More than 90 percent of the parts were manufactured in other nations such as China. They are then shipped here, to be assembled and stamped with the "Made in the USA" seal of approval, but they really aren't American cars. They are global cars, stamped with a seal of assembly.

If you sell an American-made Corvette in America, it may sell for $70,000 dollars. However, that same vehicle will sell in Europe or Japan for three times that amount. Why? Because the other nations assign an import tariff to items produced in the USA. In the meantime, we fail to do the same thing with other nations of the world. Our gates, our import and export controls, are broken down. It is time to restore them once again!

- Boeing Aircraft currently assembles a premier aircraft on both coasts of the United States. More than 90 percent of the parts come from Asia.
- The guidance systems for the "smart" bombs and missiles used by the U.S. Department of Defense are manufactured in France.
- Apple iPhones are designed and developed in the United States, but they are manufactured and assembled in China.
- Treated lumber of all types may come from the USA, but it is sent offshore to be treated. It is then returned to the

United States, and sold back to us at an inflated price. Why? Because U.S. regulations will not allow the treating process to be done on U.S. soil.

- Federal regulations prohibit coal to be used to generate electricity in the United States, in increasing levels. Instead, the coal is shipped to China, to supply their electrical demand. This demand continues to increase because U.S. manufacturing resides there.

Nehemiah and Hanani began to control the flow of merchandise through the city gates.

- They regulated the times merchandise could enter and exit.
- They regulated the vendors; no more black-market merchandise.
- They regulated the materials based on national interests instead of global pressure.

Every trade agreement enacted by the United States must be reconsidered through the lens of America-first! Every one! Furthermore, manufacturing must return to American soil as well. How can this be done? One way is by using tariffs.

Cotton shirts do not need to be manufactured in China; they can be produced in Alabama instead. If China artificially deflates the costs of the shirts using cheap labor, government incentives or volume that floods the markets, the United States must take this as an act of economic aggression. The U.S. must place tariffs on the shirts, using the money gained through tariffs to replenish Federal funds, or to help restart shuttered production and manufacturing facilities in the U.S.

Nehemiah only allowed the merchants to enter Jerusalem once the sun was high in the sky. His policies gave the local vendors inside the city walls an advantage over foreign competition. He owed nothing to the global community, and everything to the citizen. They could open early and sell to their countrymen. Every advantage should be given to America-first business. This produces solid jobs, balances the wage-scale in the nation, and affects every aspect of life (including education). Only when the sun is hot, when there is a need for something America does not or cannot produce, should the nation open her gates to external trade.

Preference must also be given to hiring U.S. citizens over refugees, immigrants or illegals that enter the land. Nehemiah certified the citizens and the non-citizens, in conjunction with regulating the gates. Business always wants and needs cheap labor, but God wants fair labor. When a nation is in covenant with God, He has promised to bless it. This means that the land will produce what it needs through the resources God has provided. Laws of supply and demand should dictate wages, not outside global forces such as external trade and the importing of outside labor.

What we have works, doesn't it?

You may not want to change the way things are working in America today. Congratulations. You are a part of the problem. Apart from food, America's primary exports today are related to entertainment, sports and the military. We import too much, and the nations of the world get richer while we get poorer. The cycle must be reversed.

The United States once produced the most advanced technology and the highest quality products in the world. Today the world looks to Asia and other nations for this type of leadership. Only when manufacturing and production returns to American soil will the innovation and quality rise once again. There will probably be things that will be forsaken during the transition period. You might have to forego that precious electronic device, or that imported gadget. In the long-term, America will prosper and so will you, but it all starts by standing up. Ayn Rand once asked a question in "Atlas Shrugged." "Who is John Galt?" Today the question must be asked, "who is Hanani?"

These were the issues that Hanani had to manage at the city gates. The walls were growing and the tide of invading illegals was soon to be stopped. The economy was being restructured, and now the flow of outside goods was being managed. It was critical for Jerusalem to bring her commerce back inside the walls if she were to survive. It is no wonder why Nehemiah chose a faithful man that feared God to manage these issues. A lesser man would be corrupted, influenced, bribed or duped. He would have left the gates open for personal gain, at the expense of the city. God, give us faithful men like Hanani today.

> *Moreover thou shalt provide out of all the people able men, such as fear God, men of truth, hating covetousness; and place such over them, to be rulers of thousands, and rulers of hundreds, rulers of fifties, and rulers of tens.* Exodus 18:21

Rule #7: Tighten the screws on commerce and leadership eligibility. No outsourcing, no foreigners in positions of power.

Questions:

- Will you be Hanani? Will you serve?
- Do you still tolerate evil in government? Why?
- Do you still tolerate foreigners in government? Why?
- What are you prepared to eliminate from your life when tariffs start?

Chapter 8 - The Laws of Nature and Nature's God

Nehemiah 8

All of the issues in Nehemiah's day, are issues faced in America today. They are spiritual in origin, yet physical in how they play out. They don't sound like spiritual issues, but they are. Things like border security. The right to keep and bear arms. The enemy within. Banking and the economy. Citizenship and outsourcing.

As with any nation rebuilding effort these are certainly the immediate concerns, but they are not the primary concern. They are just branches reaching out from a larger root. In truth, the REAL rebuilding is about to begin.

Every chapter in this book correlates to a chapter in the book of Nehemiah, found in the Bible. As you read each chapter, and then correlate it to what is written in this book, we trust that the Bible is being "normalized." Many people take natural issues found in the Bible and only "spiritualize" them. It's true, the Holy Bible is a spiritual book. But what begins in the spirit does not stay in the spirit. It takes form in the natural world. The issues presented here are just as spiritual as a creative miracle from God. So let's discuss another area where the natural world and the spiritual realm intersect.

The people of Jerusalem gathered in Nehemiah 8, to understand a critical portion of their government. It was the foundation of law. The first verse introduces us to a new player. His name is Ezra. Ezra the priest. He too writes his own book in the Bible, and he presents details of this rebuilding effort from his perspective.

"The" law

In the second verse Ezra reintroduces "the" law to the people. Notice that it is referred to as "THE" law, not just "A" law. The inference is that it is applicable to all, and there's a standard of uniformity that will be applied to everyone. Other governments may have their own laws, but what Ezra reads is more than just an ordinance passed by man. It is "the" law; the law of God Himself. It is supreme in authority, and is the common law of the nation and her people.

Here are a few observations about "THE" law in Nehemiah's day:

- "The" law was not subject to a person's "reality".
- "The" law was not the law of the Persian Empire, even though the city was technically under their jurisdiction.
- "The" law was not one that the global community had ratified.
- "The" law was the one given by God...to Moses...for the governing of all of Israel.
- It is the ONLY law for one nation under God.

Ezra's role was really quite simple. He was to bring the people back to God, and restructure their basic education system so that God was the center-point of life and society at every level.

As governor, Nehemiah applied the laws of God to the nation for its national well-being. But...

- Border security does not change a person's heart.
- The right to keep and bear arms does not change a person's heart.
- Economic reform does not change a person's heart.
- Dealing with illegal immigrants does not change a person's heart.
- Economic reforms and tariffs do not change a person's heart.

The application and understanding of "the" law, the common law, was a necessary step for the entire citizenry if the nation was going to reclaim its sovereignty and national exceptionalism.

How did he do it?

How did Ezra work to re-institute the heart changes needed? Did he do it by building a mega-church, or starting a great singles ministry? Perhaps he did it by preaching a message of relevance, and really fitting in with the culture. Right? Wrong. I know. He got a very cool Jehovah tattoo! Uh, no. Did he try to show the global community how hip he really was?

The answers are all "no."

He simply presented "the" law of God, the law designed to govern all of the nation, and instructed the people on how to conform to it.

Why Judah fell

This drills down to the core issue of why Judah fell to begin with. This is root cause for why the wall was broken down, and the reason why the people were not able to defend themselves. Why had the enemy gained a foothold from within? Why was the economy in shambles? Why were the aliens running the show? It all comes down to one simple reason. The people had rebelled against the laws of nature and of nature's God, decades before any of this happened.

For the moment, let's bring this into the present day.

Today in America, there's hardly a day that goes by without "news" of an entertainer, teacher, or politician engaging in sexual immorality. Republicans do it, Democrats do it. Men do it, women do it.

Question: Why is this so shocking to the American public, and why do we act as if this is some big surprise?

For decades we have thumbed our nose at God's virtues, and told Him He has no place in our society. We open our homes to perversion (rated G through XXX), and feast on it. We open our minds to garbage labeled as "entertainment," and watch endless hours of it on a screen. We pay good money for it, and laud the "performers" as superstars. We venerate the demon possessed or psychotic, who believe that gender is something fluid. We craft laws and policies to protect sin, and prosecute those who stand against it.

This may come as a shock to many progressives, but I self-identify as a white heterosexual male, who has sex with one woman; my wife. Not a whore, not a boyfriend, not a goat, not a girlfriend, not a partner. W.I.F.E. My gender is based on my God-given anatomy. It's not a mindset, it's my parts. Believe me, they're not fluid.

Judah got exactly what it wanted...for a while. Then, because they had weakened themselves, they fell prey to global thugs. America, what you're getting is exactly what you want...and you are trending toward the same outcome.

You have wanted politicians to redefine marriage, provide abortion on demand, no-fault divorce, and cater to your sexual appetites. So don't be shocked when they want...expect...the same favors in return. You reap what you sow.

You have wanted entertainers to offer a steady diet of illicit and immoral sex, so don't be shocked by their sexual misconduct. You reap what you sow.

You have wanted God out of the public schools. So don't be surprised when the teacher wants to have sex with your child. You reap what you sow.

You have catered to the animal instincts of your children, and rarely used the word "no." So don't be surprised when they say yes to that teacher, politician, or executive. You reap what you sow.

You have wanted a post-Christian America for decades, and now you're getting it in truckloads. Perhaps Dr. Phil needs to stand up and ask "So how's it working for you?"

If we want to remedy the problems in society, the best place to start is at home. There has been a wave of protest against the NFL because spoiled little thugs dishonor our flag and national anthem. Perhaps America would be a different place if we defended God's honor with the same zeal.

Isn't that kind of what it means to be "one nation under God?"

Yes, this is straight talk. But it's no more straight than what Ezra told the people in Nehemiah 8. Verse 9 shows that the people wept, thus indicating that they grasped the reality of their backsliding. And now, perhaps for the first time in some of their lives, they began to SEE why they had been overrun as a nation.

It was time for them to return to the laws of nature, and of nature's God.

What is the foundation?

What is the foundation of law within a culture?

- Is it the will of special interest groups or legislation?
- Is it merely the will of the people?
- Is it based on a doctrine of mutual consent?

To answer the questions, let's set this in real time and play off of current events. For example, take the issue of homosexual "marriage." Several years ago, in California, their State Supreme Court decided in favor of it. The people in the State did not even want it. They rejected it at the polls. But the courts imposed it. When that occurred, the news pundits were beating the drum on the air, showing how this local decision would impact the entire nation. Now we are there. Within the last few years, it has become "law" for the entire nation.

Four people

California's legalization of homosexual "marriage" was a decision made by 4 people; that's what constitutes a majority on the California Supreme Court. It was a decision that today impacts every person, family, business, church, patriot, and Christian citizen. It was a decision that is applauded by the sacrilegious left and all its minions…made by 4 PEOPLE!

But is that the foundation of law within a culture? Certainly the courts want you to believe so, so let's dig deeper. When California first ruled in favor of it several years prior, San Francisco Mayor Gavin Newsom stated that the courts around the nation were finally "waking up." Unfortunately, the average citizen does not realize what they were "waking up" to. They were not waking up to legal precedent that comprises the rule of law. If they were, they would have ruled AGAINST it because they have NO LEGAL FOOTING for any other decision.

History and sodomy

All 13 colonies outlawed sodomy (even committed in private) and all 50 States (including California) did as well until 1951. THAT is the legal precedent they should have measured their decision against. Instead, they sacrificed Constitutional integrity for judicial activism.

So what exactly are the courts waking up to?

- Legislation from the bench.
- Judicial overreach.

Both are unlawful.

They are shutting their eyes to the Constitution at the expense of our Republic. These modern celebrations of perversity are not the "freedom" our forefathers envisioned when they bled and died for our nation, and they were actually unlawful. Virtue was paramount, and this type of behavior was unlawful in every colony, every State. If it was not on their radar, why is it on ours?

The larger question is this; what is the foundation of law within a culture?

Is it State's rights?

The 10th Amendment crowd would tell us that it is State's rights. Played to the Nth degree...some feel that it is a State's right to choose how they define "marriage". Back when California legalized it, the 10th Amendment people said it was something you don't need to worry about since it was limited to the Granola belt... the land of fruits and nuts...the people's republic of California. That sure didn't last long, because it is now the "law" of the land.

Shouldn't communities have the right to decide their own standards? It's a question Nehemiah and Ezra had to address, so we too should look at that from a Biblical perspective. We will also look at it from a Constitutional perspective.

First the Biblical perspective, because that's the most important viewpoint.

Back to the pattern

If the issue is regarding the color they want to paint their houses, different community standards are OK. If it's an issue regarding moral standards, differing community standards are not OK. You cannot be one nation under God and have different moral standards throughout the nation. Moral law, if left up to the States, divides the nation. A house divided cannot stand. Moral law is based upon a uniform standard applicable to all.

That's why murder, rape, polygamy, child pornography, etc. are illegal in every State, county, city and township in the United States. Think of the chaos that would ensue if each State or community determined its own moral code. What if pedophilia was legalized in Kansas, but illegal in Nebraska?

God has given America the pattern in Scripture on how to be one nation under God. We don't have to look any further than His dealings with Israel to understand right and wrong nation building principles.

If you are so inclined, take a break from this book for a moment, and read the book of Judges, Chapters 19-21. There we see what happens in a nation when one State protects homosexuality and those who violently assault a traditional marriage view.

At that time, Israel consisted of 12 individual States (or tribes) with their own borders, and together they existed as one nation under God. Essentially, they were the United States of Israel. God viewed these individual States as a singular national entity, and His law did not provide an escape clause for ANY ONE State! Unfortunately for the entire nation, one tribe (or State) insisted that they could opt out of God's national moral law if it wanted to. It tried. Civil war ensued; a lot of people died.

State's rights extend only as far as the laws of God allow. No city, county, State or nation can afford to disobey the Lord. Let me remind the reader of some wise words found in Deuteronomy 28.

Deuteronomy 28:1-2 – *And it shall come to pass, if thou shalt hearken diligently unto the voice of the LORD thy God, to observe and to do all his commandments which I command thee this day, that the LORD thy God will set thee on high above all nations of the earth: And all these blessings shall come on thee, and overtake thee, if thou shalt hearken unto the voice of the LORD thy God.*

While we can apply that principle to individuals, families, churches, businesses, etc., its real potency is felt when we see it in its national context. This is a promise given to a nation who is established to be one nation under God. This passage promises NATIONAL INEQUALITY, NATIONAL EXCEPTIONALISM. It promises an unequal outcome for the nation who puts God first. God will put THEM first. So much for God being a socialist.

America was not made great by men who envisioned us being a trash can for celebrations of perversion. It was made great because our core was centered on the Lord Jesus Christ, and our laws and culture have reflected that. Until recently. We are foolish to herald our new-found "enlightenment" as progress, and the only hope for America is if we repent. We must return to the laws of nature and of nature's God. There is no other way! Absolutely none!

Consenting adults

The question could be asked, *if it is done between consenting adults, why not allow it?*

Once again, that argument is based on a misunderstanding of the rule of law. The Kingdom of God operates on the rule of law. "The" law always maintains a standard of uniformity that everyone must conform to, everyone must obey. "The" law is rigid, and the people must bend to conform to it. People must change their behavior to conform to that framework, not seek to alter that framework to fit their appetites.

You and your spouse cannot decide today that it's OK to exceed the speed limit, and then expect the officer to understand that the decision was made between consenting adults, and let you off the hook. Why? The law always takes precedent in a civilized society, not a personal or corporate agenda that challenges the law.

If you believe that mutual consent is the foundation of law within a culture, here is something to ponder. Should the local chapter of the goddess moonbeam, be allowed to perform a human sacrifice, to appease mother earth, if all parties give their consent? After all, everything is being done between consenting adults! If you say "no", yet you cling to the "consenting adult" argument, you are being hypocritical. Where will you draw the line?

Mutual consent opens up a Pandora's Box of anarchy, because you will ALWAYS be able to find two people who give their consent to something, no matter how perverse or aberrant it may be.

This is why Judah fell prior to Nehemiah's time, and it the same reason that America is in the State she is in today. Thankfully, the people under Nehemiah had a willingness to hear…and do… the laws of God.

But wait. There's more.

We have looked at this from a Biblical perspective, but let's examine it from the Constitutional perspective for a moment.

Article 4 Section 1 of the Constitution reads in part…"*Full faith and credit shall be given in each State to the public acts, records, and judicial proceedings of every other State…*"

The ripple effect of one State's decision can be staggering and have unintended consequences across the entire nation. When the push was on for localized homosexual "marriage", we told our listeners on the In Defense of a Nation radio broadcast that homosexual activists had no intention of leaving it localized. They only *said* it should be a local decision to seduce the rest of the nation into a state of slumber and inactivity. They knew full well that it would create the foundation to force it down every other State's throat. Even those in the "Bible Belt."

At some point, your business, your church, your child's school, will be sued by homosexual activists to honor the public acts and records of California. They will do so on the authority of the Constitution, though the original ruling was a complete abrogation of legal precedent. The enemy within will pick and choose which laws they revere, which laws they attack, and when to apply those laws against their enemies. That means you!

When that occurs, America will be FORCED by a noisy evil minority to adopt a morality and policy not created by the voters, and abhorred by God. It will be illegal to speak out against it because it will be legal and protected behavior! People of faith will be criminalized for standing against it.

Take a stand, and speak up anyway.

Needed: Ezra.

Who do we need today? We need for Ezra to stand up once again and declare "the" law to America. We're not talking about the law that is in place, because it can be used selectively to abuse and impose corruption at every level. We need the laws of nature and of nature's God to be painted all over the public square once again. How can we do this?

First, the Holy Bible must be reinstated as the common law of the United States of America. Long before the colonies had agreements with each other, each one had a Bible. The towns and colonies used the Bible as their foundation, their law-book, to try cases, agree on procedures and punishments, and try crimes within the civil and criminal courts of the colonies of America.

When the colonies gained their independence they bound themselves together using the United States Constitution. However, the Constitution was only approved when ratified with the first ten articles of the Bill of Rights. These ten articles were rooted in Scripture, and protected the rights of the people and the States. Over time we have kept the Constitution and the Bill of Rights, but we have forsaken the Common Law that held it all together. It is time for a Constitutional amendment that recognizes the fact that all law within the U.S. must conform to her common law, the Holy Bible.

Second, the law must be taught in public once again. The Bible must be reintroduced into the classrooms of every public school. It must be taught as the moral foundation, the code by which America lives and thrives. The first textbook used in public schools in the colonies was the Bible. It must be reclaimed and used in public school once again.

Third, all laws at every strata of government must be reevaluated and checked, to see if they conform to the common law, the Bible. This will demand biblical expertise. There are 1,189 chapters in the Bible. America needs experts in these chapters that can compare his or her chapter to the law in question. These laws can be approved or denied, based on their conformity to "the" law. Courts can compare their rulings to "the" law as well.

It is time to return to the laws of nature and nature's God. It is time to return to the Bible as "the" law in America. That is the real foundation of the wall, the second amendment, and every other liberty cherished by man.

And it shall come to pass, if thou shalt hearken diligently unto the voice of the Lord thy God, to observe and to do all his commandments which I command thee this day, that the Lord thy God

will set thee on high above all nations of the earth.
Deuteronomy 28:1

Rule #8: Make the Holy Bible the common law of the United States of America. Every other law and statute must conform to it, or be rendered invalid.

Questions:

- What moral foundation do you live by? What needs to change?
- The founders of the United States studied the Old Testament to understand how to build a nation and a moral society. What do you study?
- What will you do to implement the Bible as the law? In business? In education? In government?

Chapter 9 - Reclaiming the American Story

Nehemiah 9

James

James is a church-going Christian man that sits on the local school board, overseeing the education of 20,000 students. When a group presented an elective curriculum that taught the role of the Bible in American history and literature, James rejected it. Why? He was concerned that it was not multicultural enough.

Adam

Adam pastors a megachurch, and is a gifted speaker and author. He too opposes inserting the Bible into public school. He won't say so from his pulpit, but behind the scenes he makes calls to oppose other pastors that seek to reinsert the Bible into public areas like schools and colleges. He believes the Bible should be taught mainly at home, and by pastors in churches. He ignores groups like the Gideons (one of the largest Bible distribution groups in the world) when they call him, and tends to focus on other issues such as social justice and equal outcome.

Kristina

Kristina is a mother that attends the church Adam pastors. Her three children love the children's ministry there, and she likes how Adam teaches. She has been growing increasingly concerned about her oldest two children, because their lives are beginning to reflect the values of current society. They talk about the current issues of society and generally agree with their peers about issues like social justice and gender fluidity. Her children spend every week in public schools, and every weekend in church. What could possibly be wrong?

Ramond

Ramond is a pastor and missionary that has traveled to more than 50 nations of the world. He has seen people come to Christ around the world, and ministers out of the church he pastors in the United States. He readily acknowledges that the U.S. stands head and shoulders above every other nation he has visited. This is why he supports open borders for immigrants. He also believes that nations are largely equal. When asked why the U.S. is blessed above all nations, he thinks that it may be because America supports the Jews or that we "just got lucky." He tends to shy away from issues like this in the pulpit, because people want to hear about how to live their lives today. They don't want to deal with those kinds of things.

Kevin

Kevin is a solid husband and dad that doesn't bother attending church with his wife and children. Sometimes he shows up around Christmas or Easter, but other than that he lives a different life. Kevin is a patriot that stands when the national anthem is played. He dislikes most politicians as a general rule, and ranks most pastors one step below them. He tries to raise his family to love liberty, country, and God. In fact, Kevin lets his wife Kathy take the children to church even though he doesn't attend himself. He thinks Pastor Adam is spineless, and only seeks to appease. He privately calls him a squish. He will readily tell you that America is the greatest nation on earth, and he will exercise his second-amendment rights to keep her free and strong, but he sees no connection between God and country. Nobody has ever showed him the connection.

> *Nehemiah 9:1 - Now in the twenty and fourth day of this month the children of Israel were assembled with fasting, and with sackclothes, and earth upon them.*

In our previous chapter we covered the necessity of repentance, turning back to the laws of nature, and of nature's God. The people did it in Nehemiah's day, and it restored the nation. Is there a "why" behind "what" they are doing, that extends beyond what they have suffered as a nation? History shows that a tectonic shift was underway in Judah, as illustrated in the next verse.

> *Nehemiah 9:2 - And the seed of Israel separated themselves from all strangers, and stood and confessed their sins, and the iniquities of their fathers.*

Separation from the strangers (the global community), those who held no allegiance to the laws of God vested into Israel's culture, reveals how big this national shift really is. Why are they doing this?

In verses 7-13, the leaders revisited the history of their people at their founding, to remind them of who they are today. They literally took the time to celebrate who they were *at the beginning of their nation.* THAT is their real identity! Who they have become as a nation today, must actually snap back toward this plumb line if they want to make their nation great again.

This is not the celebration of diversity that the global community swoons over. It is a celebration of their founding heritage. Since the fallacy of global equivalency has run its course, and destroyed Judah's sovereignty, there must be a renewal of their national identity. This is why Judah separates itself from the global community that has walked all over it for decades.

Celebrate our founding heritage

America must celebrate her founding heritage, the heritage that God has given her. In spite of every attempt by the global community to redefine who we are, nobody can take away our foundation. Even UN resettlement strategies designed to dilute us and pollute us, cannot take away our foundation. The rule for rebuilders is this: Reclaim America's history!

Two of the most protested holidays in America are Thanksgiving and Columbus Day. There is even a concerted effort to counter Columbus Day with National Indigenous People Day. But consider this; in 1487, five years before Columbus arrived, the Aztecs sacrificed as many as eighty four thousand men, women, and children at the re-consecration of the Great Pyramid of Tenochtitlan. Is that something worth celebrating? If you are still drinking the Kool-Aid of cultural equivalency, spin us on the reason to celebrate Indigenous People's Day again. We don't see much cause for celebration over the practices of some cultures, but we do find cause to celebrate the conquest of this land by Europeans, *"for the glory of God and for the advancement of the Christian faith."* You will find those words in the Mayflower Compact. And no, it was not a global compact.

Conquered peoples, and their ill-informed sympathizers should remember that the history of humanity is one of constant conflict and competition for resources: resources like land, food, and water. It even consists of God...yes, God...instructing His people to uproot indigenous people groups, and take their land. Like it or not, the cold hard fact is that Europeans were, and still are, better at this contest than any other race in the world. They are the reason America exists and prospers today, and that is worth celebrating.

If you believe that national regret for our existence is America's path forward to greatness, think again. Apologies and reparations from people who are better at conquest and exploration, people who conquered by the hand of God, people who unequivocally won, must be taken off the table. Nehemiah had to address this in his time, and it's time we did it again in America. Today. There must be an unapologetic celebration of our cultural and Christ-centered foundation. This may come as a shock to progressives, but when the Pilgrims boarded the Mayflower, and set sail to establish the new world, Buddha was not on the boat. Neither was Muhammad. Neither was Stalin.

Like Judah, America was founded as one nation under ONE God. Prior to Nehemiah's leadership, Judah had not recognized that for decades. But Nehemiah brought them back around to that truth. Then the entire nation had to embrace it once again.

What do you believe?

Do you believe the myth of global equivalency? Do you believe in national equality? Indulge us for a moment as we take a virtual trip around the world for the sake of discovery. America is unique in human history, so there must be something special about us. Progressives may say otherwise, and insist that we are one among equals, but nothing in history supports that fallacy.

Furthermore, that lie is contrary to the Bible. We closed the last chapter with a Bible verse that we might want to read again.

> *And it shall come to pass, if thou shalt hearken dili-gently unto the voice of the Lord thy God, to observe and to do all his commandments which I command thee this day, that the Lord thy God will set thee on high above all nations of the earth: and all these blessings shall come on thee, and overtake thee, if thou shalt hearken unto the voice of the Lord thy God.* Deuteronomy 28:1-2

This verse makes several critical points.

- God does not treat all nations equally. Some are blessed; others are not.
- God elevates a nation with prosperity if they build upon His commandments.
- Every nation is built upon a religious framework. Every one. The God (or god) that nation chooses will either bring a blessing, or a curse.

So much for cultural equivalency.

Let's look at a few nations

Consider for a moment the "Islamic Republic of Iran." It is the pinnacle of what islam can build into a nation. The law is based on sharia, and what allah has to offer. Has it prospered? No. Is there equal opportunity offered to women? No. Are Christians free to worship? No. Is there freedom of the Press? No. Has it fed the world, and extended a helping hand during times of crisis? No.

How about the former "United States of the Soviet Republic?" It is the pinnacle of what humans can build into a nation when they defy God. Did it prosper? No. Was there unhindered opportunity to pursue life, liberty, and happiness? No. Were Christians free to worship? No. Was there freedom of the Press? No. In spite of its vast resources, was it the breadbasket of the world, filling it with food and freedom? No.

Ah, I know...let's try India, the birthplace for much of the "New Age" philosophy that has taken hold in the West. You can choose to sacrifice to one of a million gods. There is no heaven, no hell, and if you don't get it right the first time, you may come back as a cow in another life. Aunt Betty may actually be that heifer grazing in the field, so you may starve before you eat that steak. But that aside, let's ask similar questions. Has the nation prospered? No. Is there liberty for all to prosper? No. Are Christians free to worship? No.

Starting to sound familiar?

Let's try one more. The buddhists want a nation of their own. This is the point behind the "free Tibet" movement. China is built on a framework of Taoism and Communism, where the State is god. Need we continue, or do you get the point? In our quick little virtual trip, we have certainly discovered who we are NOT. We are not of this world. Nothing about America was shaped by global ideas that are wrecking other nations today.

- America is not islam.
- America is not buddhism.
- America is not communism.
- America is not socialism.
- America is not new age philosophy.
- America is not humanism.
- America is not statism.

America is a national expression of one faith and one God... Christianity and the Lord Jesus Christ. This nation had no national church, but she embraced a national faith. Consider this for a moment.

- The first Christian churches founded by the colonies were started in 1610 and 1620, in Jamestown, Virginia and Plymouth, Massachusetts.
- The first Jewish synagogue in America was built in 1763, in Newport, Rhode Island.
- The first buddhist temple in America was built in 1853, in San Francisco, California.
- The first muslim mosque in America was built in 1934, in Cedar Rapids, Iowa.
- The first hindu temple in America was built in 1970, in Flushing, Queens, New York.

Four out of those five religions and cultures did not build America. Only one did; Christianity.

Anyone with any sense can see the destruction that other philosophies and religions bring. Islam is the latest fad in America, but it is not embraced because of what it produces. Any neutral observer remotely interested in facts can see that it is destructive beyond words. Yet because of our dislike for Christian virtues and restraints, it is being embraced as a form of protest against our Christian heritage. That is the only reason it is venerated by ignorant Westerners. A muslim woman in an islamic country has no freedom of speech. So when she protests here, to advocate sharia law, she is using free speech to ask that we take away her free speech. Get the picture? Westerners embracing islam have lost their minds.

Nehemiah did not gather Judah for a group hug with the global community. He gathered them to celebrate who they were in their founding. And in that, he had to exclude other faiths.

They were one nation under one God, not one nation under every god.

Looking ahead, America must learn to hate islam. That is not to say that we hate muslims, but we must hate islam. Why? Islam is a political system set on ruling the globe, overthrowing our Constitutional Republic, and the Christian faith we are built upon. It is not compatible with America. And if God hates islam, shouldn't His people? These are the implications if we are to be one nation under God.

Bad theology; horrible policy

Tommy was raised in a minister's home that focused largely on global equality. They believed in Almighty God, but also felt that all philosophies and religions could coexist. As Tommy progressed through college, he was increasingly influenced by globalists in education and society. Eventually Tommy became known by a different name, and inserted his philosophies of "Christian globalism" into the government of the United States of America. Tommy is actually Thomas Woodrow Wilson. His globalist Christian views opened the door for the Federal Reserve, false currency, and the predecessor to the U.N., the League of Nations.

When we begin to believe that everything can coexist, and that all nations with all gods are co-equal, we fail.

The truth of the matter

The United States of America was founded upon the Bible, Jesus Christ, Almighty God, and the moral laws that emanated from that. Many people today will try to tell you that America is like Rome, Greece, or other ancient nations. They are wrong. These nations had Christianity introduced from the outside to a pagan culture that already existed.

The United States was built upon the Bible from the inside-out.

- The first government buildings in America were Christian churches.
- The Mayflower Compact declares that we are to be established for "the glory of God and the advancement of the Christian faith."
- The Declaration of Independence references the Christian God repeatedly.
- The U.S. Constitution endorses Christianity in two specific places. No other religion is recognized.
- The first ten articles of the Bill of Rights are linked to Bible verses, guaranteeing liberties to the people of the United States.
- The three branches of U.S. government were first discovered in Isaiah 33:22.
- The concept of Federal, State, county and city government is rooted in Exodus 18:21.
- Dr. Benjamin Rush, the founder of the public school system in America, published a pamphlet sharing 15 reasons why the Bible was the primary textbook in America's public schools.
- The backbone of American government was built upon William Blackstone's "Commentaries on the Laws of England." His commentaries on law are filled with Scriptures and Bible examples.
- The father of free-market economics was a Christian philosopher named Adam Smith. His book, "Wealth of Nations" became the economic engine that helped propel America to prosperity and blessing, the Bible way.

Buddha was not here. Mohammed was considered a barbarian. Other religions were failures. The United States of America was founded upon the Bible and Almighty God.

For further study

Every patriot, Christian and lover of America should dig deeply into this defining issue that made America great. For starters, we recommend the following materials for further study.

- *America in the Bible* - by Steven Grant
- *Why America Still Matters to God* - by Geoffery Broughton
- *The Bible is the Higher Law in America* - by Tom Hughes
- *The 5,000 Year Leap* - by W. Cleon Skousen
- *Christianity and the American Commonwealth* - by Charles B. Galloway
- *The United States: A Christian Nation* - by former U.S. Supreme Court Associate Justice David J. Brewer
- *The American Heritage* DVD Series - by David Barton
- *Monumental* DVD - by Kirk Cameron

The "why" behind the "what"

Nehemiah 9 shows that Judah celebrated who they were in their beginnings, not what they had become. They celebrated their national relationship with God, and the outflow of that prompted political action!

- Why build the wall? Because of who they are...and who God was to their nation.
- Why is their land sovereign? Because of who they are... and who God was to their nation.
- Why upend the economic system? Because of who they are...and who God was to their nation.

- Why abandon globalism? Because of who they are...and who God was to their nation.
- Why reform education? Because of who they are...and who God was to their nation.
- Why re-establish the true foundation of law within the culture? Because of who they are...and who God was to their nation.
- Why challenge the enemy within? Because of who they are...and who God was to their nation.

This is not a story about David, Sampson, Gideon, or any other event-centered story about the patriarchs. That's because rebuilding a nation is not anchored to events. It is anchored to identity. Identity doesn't come from UN headquarters, it comes from God! Identity does not come from what we embrace now, it comes from what we embraced at our founding. And that is what drives the change in politics!!

If you don't know who you are, and who God is to your nation, the whole concept of "one nation under God" is just another good idea that can change based on current whims of the prevailing culture. It becomes a good but antiquated idea that can then be relegated to the dustbins of history. But if it is more than that, if we are joined in Covenant with our Creator, the "one nation under God" concept is a binding issue that obligates us to serving Him nationally. And there's a cost associated with that.

For Judah, they connected to this understanding and concept, and it cost them every progressive concept they were holding on to. This is why the enemy within fought Nehemiah from the start. Progressivism DIES when you realize who you are, and who God is to your nation. This progressivism is at the root of their sins... and their judgment. It's the common idiocy of keeping up with the Jones'...the national Jones'. It's the mindset that "if other nations are doing it, perhaps we should embrace it". That's the insanity that brought the nation to a place of ruin. This is what is being reversed in Nehemiah 9, by celebrating their founding heritage.

Once America rediscovers who it really is, THAT will become the driving force behind our NATIONAL actions. Historical revisionism has cost us a true picture of who we truly are. Like Judah, we must realize who we were created to be, what national obligations we have to God, and the covenant between Heaven and our nation. There's power in that revelation, enough power to change our nation! Once we embrace that, we will become largely unconcerned with the opinions of the global community! Judah stopped caring about the global pursuits of nations around them. The knowledge of their true identity is what gave them the STRENGTH to be what GOD had called them to be.

Focusing on the present, the crux of the American experience is no different. America is being told who it is by talking heads in the UN and DC. Because of that, we've forgotten who we are. We believe the revisionists, whether they be in the media, politics, pulpits, or Hollywood.

The mere existence of America is a story worth celebrating, as well as our national relationship with God. True, we are misbehaving badly right now, and God cannot turn a blind eye to our behavior much longer. BUT, behavior is not the key ingredient in determining one's core identity.

In our family, we will always be Grant boys regardless of our behavior. How we act today does not change who we are. Judah of old had bad behavior and administrations, yet that did not change their IDENTITY or God's ownership of them. It got them into a mess, but they were still one nation under God.

Real America

REAL America (in contrast to revisionist America) stands in stark contrast to any other system in the world today. It even stands in stark contrast to the system of antichrist as outlined in Scripture.

- Real America is humanitarian. The system of the beast is abusive.
- Real America is benevolent. We often extend loans without demanding payback. The system of the beast is oppressive.
- In real America, churches dot the landscape from sea to shining sea. The system of the beast assaults the Christian faith.
- Real America is the greatest missions-sending nation in the history of the world. The system of the beast exhibits a hatred for Christianity.
- Real America fills the world with food. Under the beast system, you can't even buy or sell without its mark.
- Real America is about freedom of religion, freedom of speech, peaceable assembly, freedom of the Press, and the right to keep and bear arms. Under the beast system, you have no such rights.

This does not describe a nation birthed and conceived in hell, regardless of how bad our behavior or administration is today. We do not exist as an afterthought in the courts of Heaven. America does not exist because a few Christian pilgrims got lucky and hit the Christian Nation jackpot. America exists by design...divine design...and American patriots intuitively know that how we are acting today is not who we really are.

We ARE one nation under God, and if you remove America from the picture, the world has major problems. That is precisely what the system of antichrist wants. It yearns for a one-world "problem" that allows it to impose its one-world "solution." It wants to degrade and weaken America so it can have its way, but it is time to celebrate and reaffirm who we really are. That will become the motivation behind the actions we must undertake!

- Build the wall! Because of who we are...and who God is to our nation.
- This land is ours! Because of who we are...and who God is to our nation.
- Upend the current economic system! Because of who we are...and who God is to our nation.
- Reform education! Because of who we are...and who God is to our nation.
- Abandon globalism! Because of who we are...and who God is to our nation.
- Challenge the enemy within! Because of who we are...and who God is to our nation.

In case you were unaware, this is why leftists (in both parties) are so dangerous to America. Their disdain for our nation is grounded in contempt for who we are, and who God is to our nation. And this is precisely why those who are right cannot afford to remain silent. The political battles being waged are merely a cloak for the spirit behind it that wants to take us apart, and the more we celebrate who we truly are, the more it exposes the enemy within.

I have news for America; they will not succeed! Global efforts brought to bear against America will FAIL...because of who we are, and who God is to our nation. Dust off the history book, and dust off your voice. It is time to reclaim the American story!

...and it shall come to pass, that in the place where it was said unto them, Ye are not my people, there it shall be said unto them, Ye are the sons of the living God. Hosea 1:10

Rule #9: Reclaim America's History!

Questions:

- What do you believe about America? Are we equal to all nations or not? What implications does your belief system have?
- Are you willing to stand up and work to reclaim America? What do you need to learn?
- Where do you need to start reclaiming America?

Chapter 10 - The State Is Not God

Nehemiah 10

Have you been reading through Nehemiah along with this book? No, really! If you have, you have encountered a few lists of names by this time. They are lists of collaborators, enemies, government leaders, and citizens. Today we add yet another list to the pile, and it really does matter why it is even there!

As we read the story of Nehemiah and his nation (The House of Judah), in spite of the trouble they have experienced because of their own doing, chapter 10 shows them starting to turn the corner. Once again, we will apply this to the rules God has given to the United States of America. If we follow the pattern, America will be made great again. If not, America will continue to fail.

Until now most of the authority has been consolidated into the hands of a few trusted men, including Nehemiah. In this chapter a critical decision is made, and with it comes a *renewed separation of powers*. It is directly connected to the laws of God, vested in all levels of authority. Until now it has only been discussed. Now it is put into action.

Authority

In order to be blessed by Almighty God we must understand how He administers authority in the world. God delegates authority to us for various spheres of life. The husband is the leader of the home. The sheriff is the highest law enforcement authority in the county. The President is given authority over the executive branch of the nation, and so on. Within this authority we have the ability to do right, or do wrong. God did NOT stop Adam and Eve from sinning. He did not stop wicked kings from ruling as tyrants. He enabled mankind to create checks and balances, to repel tyranny, and to overthrow the wicked. God allows each of us to obey or rebel. He does not revoke His authority, because mankind is created in the image of God to have and exercise authority on the earth. Therefore, it is up to us to either exercise God's moral, biblical authority voluntarily, or live in alliance with the rulers of the darkness of this world. We decide.

Nehemiah began chapter 10 by listing the signers of the covenant, the constitution, with Almighty God.

- The Mayflower Compact has the names of its signers.
- The Declaration of Independence bears the names of its signers.
- The U.S. Constitution carries the names of its signers.

With every fresh resurgence of liberty and mutual commitment, it is up to the leaders to sign on to the covenant.

The first signer in Nehemiah 10 was Nehemiah himself, as the governor of the nation. *"Now those that sealed were, Nehemiah, the Tirshatha, the son of Hachaliah…"* Nehemiah 10:1 He signed a covenant, uniting the nation with Almighty God, as the head of the nation. But the list doesn't stop there. Next were the princes. This was followed by the Levites, and priests.

Simply put, these were all the leaders in the society. It included national leaders and spiritual leaders alike. Their fresh resolve to follow God's law was put into constituted form and signed with their own hands.

Government under God

Verses 2-8 detailed all the other "princes" or governmental leaders tasked with the powers of government. Each of these governmental leaders now signed onto a constitution uniting the nation with Almighty God, and Him alone.

- We are not told about their personal spiritual beliefs.
- Nothing is said about their commitment to diversity.
- Their viewpoints about global warming, social justice, feminism, and the spotted owl are not documented.

What IS recorded however, is their firm resolve to place the nation under the all-seeing eye of Almighty God. This would be equivalent to every national governmental official signing a pact with God.

- Every Congressman.
- Every Senator.
- The President.
- Every cabinet member.
- Every Federal Judge.
- The members of the U.S. Supreme Court.

All of them.

When the Mayflower was blown off course in November, 1620, the colonists on board knew that they were far from the Virginia region. They would have to start a unique colony of their own. Part of the colony was comprised of a strong, godly core of pilgrims. They were known as "the saints." Others, such as Miles Standish, had come seeking adventure. They believed in Almighty God, but they were not seeking to build a religious colony. They wanted to seek their fortunes in the new land. These colonists were referred to as "the strangers." William Bradford had been appointed to be their governor, but he knew there was no common fabric to knit the colony together. So together, he and the others aboard the Mayflower drafted the most significant governing document in the American colonies. It became known as the Mayflower Compact. That document lists the specific intent of the Mayflower voyage, and colony.

"Having undertaken, for the glory of God, and advancements of the Christian faith..."

All of the men aboard the Mayflower signed the Compact. All of them. The saints and the strangers alike. They bound the colony to Almighty God with a covenant, and it produced the most successful colony in early American history.

While all of this might have been "new" to the culture as it existed in Nehemiah's time, this bold fresh move was really something quite "old". It was a return to the old paths, the law of God as given to Moses. And they put it in constituted form.

After the governmental leaders signed on to the covenant, it was time for the spiritual leaders to step up. They are listed in verses 9-27. Their names are important, because they provided the moral and educational spine of the nation. The priests and levites were in charge of running the synagogues (churches), the temple, all of the schools, and every charitable and social organization in the nation. These people had to return to a covenant with Almighty God themselves!

The welfare State

We could talk about how to institute this, but instead let's focus on the results in Nehemiah's day. It is seen starting in verse 32. The people bring their offerings of charity and tithes to the church. Not the State, the church. No big deal, right? Wrong. Until this time, the State had taxed at-will, and administered welfare at-will. This role, and the associated charitable giving is severed from government. It is reclaimed by the church and religious leaders.

What is important about this step? For the first time in decades, the State is minimized, and discovers that it is not God.

Huge.

To make a nation great again, it is necessary for EVERYONE to adopt this mindset. The final corporate balance of power against an overreaching State is that of the church. State welfare systems only create slaves, and history is full of ancient and modern examples.

- Egypt and Pharaoh vs. Israel. Initially, Israel was taken care of. Then they were enslaved by an overreaching State.
- Persia vs. Daniel and the three Hebrew children. Initially Daniel and the three Hebrew children were cared for, but then an unaccountable State sought to completely enslave them, even to the extent of what they believed. The three Hebrew children walked through the fire, and Daniel survived the lion's den, but both events came at the hands of State overreach.
- Judah vs. Jesus. If you want a great picture of a kangaroo court, look no further than the Jews' "trial" of Jesus. They hated His version of charity, and killed Him for it. Just another example of a State which believed that IT was God.
- The former USSR. How about 30 million Christians killed under Stalin? Those who acquiesced and worshiped the government were "cared for", but the State could not tolerate a God other than itself.

For Nehemiah and the leaders, taking charity from the government, and putting it back in the hands of the church, was a pivotal step in rightly defining the State's role.

Today, most charity isn't charity. Much charity is profiteering under non-profit status. Much charity is governmental operations under the guise of a religious group. Other charity operates under the guise of doing good, without God.

Consider many of the fake-charities that operate today. They have religious names, and even claim to work to help the downtrodden and needy. In all reality, they are liberal, globalist, government organizations. Who are we talking about? Catholic Charities. More than 80 percent of their funding comes from the government; not from the Catholic Church. They are a fake charity. Then there is Lutheran Services. Again, more than 80 percent funded by the government. They are deeply involved in bringing in and resettling muslim "refugees." These are just two examples of charities operating as religious organizations, while largely doing work for the government. A recent study of charities across the U.S. shows that 25 percent of their annual, recurring funding comes from the government. This is in addition to the grants they receive, the programs they run, services for which they are reimbursed, and other hidden revenues. This is not welfare or other social spending! These are charities!

Many hospitals are still operated as religious, non-profit organizations, but they make a healthy profit. Lutheran hospitals continues to acquire and grow into a massive non-profit hospital system. We can guarantee you it's not about charity for the individual, but profits for the bottom line. Most universities were started as private, religious institutions. Today, most of them are bastions of liberal garbage, receiving hundreds of millions in grants and fundings from government. These cords must be severed, and government must get out of nearly all facets of charity, social spending, and various entitlement programs that keep the masses looking to government as god.

Divide the spending

Nehemiah's government didn't just downsize. It restructured completely, and cut power and operations by more than half! Government reverted back to God's parameters, and opened the door for the church to play the role that God had ordained it to take. For the government:

- Power was removed.
- Spending was slashed.
- Bureaucrats were no longer needed.
- Purse strings were cut.
- People were forced to look away from it for help, and look to the church...and God.

Many often debate about the roles of church and State, but Nehemiah defined them. The State handled national security, the judicial branch, economic liberty and the guarantee of just weights and measures, and liberty for religion under Almighty God's parameters. Under his leadership, the State acknowledged that it operated UNDER Almighty God; not AS Almighty God!

The State was relieved of all social programs. Welfare spending? Gone! Education? Now under the leadership of the church once again, including all of the universities. Medical spending? Privatized. Charity? No government funds involved! It was all divested from government, and placed into the hands of the church.

You may try to argue the points made in this chapter because "government needs to handle these things in order to be administered fairly." There are several fallacies with that argument. We will name a couple of them. First, most people want the government to handle things, because they don't want to take responsibility.

It's not just welfare. It's the parents, with their child's education. It's the citizen that votes every four years and then ignores every city council meeting. The fact is this; most Americans don't want to have to work hard, to reclaim America. It's time to get off of lazy rear ends and change that!

Do you worship Saul Alinsky, or God?

The second reason most people want the government to control these areas is because of the work of one man. His name? Saul Alinsky. Alinsky's book, "Rules for Radicals" became a defining work in the 1970's. Birthed out of the rebellion of the 1960's Alinsky dedicated his book to lucifer, and sought to tear down every vestige of Christian America. How? He sought to bring most of the key influencing areas of life and society under the control of the government. Among these areas were education, charity and social spending, and medicine! (Note: His intent in doing this was to destroy Christian America, and make the State into god.)

Today, most Christians are more closely aligned with Alinsky than with God. Alinsky though has become the norm, so it is no longer challenged. Many do not realize that they're embracing Marxist ideology. They would condemn Nehemiah and embrace the workings of lucifer, and that includes many pastors. Many in the church need to repent and relearn how the Bible works, but that would demand humility, honesty, and work.

WDND?

So what did Nehemiah do? He limited the authority of government. He brought it back to a smaller, leaner, more focused operation. He divested the roles of education, charity, social spending away from the government. This was given to the levites, the educators, pastors, and executives of charitable work. Today, this would include:

- All schools.
- All universities.
- All hospitals.
- All charities.
- All welfare.
- All medicare and medicaid.
- All social security.
- All school food programs, etc., etc., etc.

Do you get the picture?

Can it work?

If you think this cannot work, you are wrong. It has worked well, and more efficiently than any program in use today. It worked effectively in Nehemiah's time, so much so that the people voluntarily passed taxation, not for the State, but for the church! The government had reined in spending to a maximum of 10 percent taxation! This enabled the people to tithe to their church and contribute to charities. They gave to charity at a huge level because they recognized the responsibility, and were committed as much to God and the church as they were to the State!

During the mid-1800's, the United States became blessed and prosperous. During this season nearly all hospitals were funded by church-based charities. The vast majority of the schools were still church-run. Nearly every university in America was operated by churches and denominations. There were soup kitchens, boarding houses, charitable operations in nearly every city, and groups like the Young Men's Christian Association (YMCA) had sprung up to offer low-cost housing to young men migrating to cities to find work. All of this was done with private, charitable giving. It was so successful that the charitable giving in the United States exceeded the entire budget of the Federal government! It has worked before. It will work again.

"Ye are cursed with a curse; for ye have robbed me, even this whole nation. Bring ye all the tithes into the storehouse, that there may be meat in mine house, and prove me now herewith, saith the Lord of hosts, if I will not open you the windows of heaven, and pour you out a blessing, that there shall not be room enough to receive it." Malachi 3:9-10

Rule #10: Separate social programs and charitable spending from government.

Questions:

- Do you agree with Alinsky, or God?
- What segment of society will you work on, as it is freed from government control?
- How will education, charity and medicine restructure as it is detached from government, and placed under the oversight of the church?

Chapter 11 - Immigration, God's Way

Nehemiah 11

With God's help, Nehemiah has made Jerusalem great again. Commerce has returned to the heart of the Jewish State of Israel. Their identity as a people has been validated with the reconstruction of the city walls. The economy has been reformed, the border is secure, their identity has been reclaimed, and the nation is coming on strong.

Chapter 11 of Nehemiah details those who returned to the city of Jerusalem versus those who remained in the outer cities. Jerusalem was the center, the heartbeat of the nation. Living in Jerusalem would be a sacrifice, an act of service. It was both an honor and a responsibility to dwell there. Governmental leaders, military personnel, chief priests, business leaders, skilled musicians and other leaders were selected and honored to live in Jerusalem. It was intended to be the crown jewel of a nation that embraced covenant life under Almighty God. That's why they had to draw straws to see who could dwell there. Space was limited...and not everyone could get in. Simply being a dreamer did not qualify you for admittance, and every policy clearly swung towards nationalism. Policies now decisively catered to the founding elements of the culture; revisionism and globalism were abandoned as the failed experiments that they were. The nation no longer existed as a doormat for world powers, it was no longer a globalist-friendly environment.

The national census

In order to select those that would live in Jerusalem, there had to be a reckoning of the people; a national census of sorts. Not everyone that *wanted* to live in Jerusalem *could* live in Jerusalem. Immigration and migration policies now had to be implemented for the nation.

God had given Israel His immigration policies, but to their detriment, they had abandoned them long ago. Globalists and the cultures of the world were enabled to coexist on an equal footing with Almighty God. Enemies of liberty like Sanballat, Tobiah and Geshem had been elevated to high positions, prior to the arrival of Nehemiah. They had been displaced in the new government, but the seeds of coexistence were still rampant throughout the nation. Now it is being stopped. Cold.

If you move to India, you will be forced to accept the prevailing culture, language, religion and heritage. Colonists are not embraced. You must assimilate, and you must accept what is there.

- If you move to Mexico, you must comply with Mexican authority and law.
- If you move to Iran, you must accept life under an islamic regime.
- If you move to China, you will live under communism.

If you were to move to Jerusalem in Nehemiah's time, you would be required to learn the language, embrace Almighty God as your own, recognize the Jews as the leaders of the land, and submit to the laws, structure and government within that framework. The United States must do the same!

By chapter 11, it was clear who the citizens of this nation truly were. It was also obvious who the outsiders were, who the enemies were, and what their agendas were. The land may have been a blessing for them, but they were not a blessing to the land. They were consumers, living self-centered lives, taking from the kingdom without making a full commitment to the culture, language, religion and lifestyle. God hated this then, and He hates it now! It was time for Immigration reform, God's way.

God has an immigration plan that works

Most Americans think that immigration policy is a political issue. It is not. Immigration policy is actually a biblical issue. God had a plan for immigration when he established the nations.

> *"When the most High divided to the nations their inheritance, when he separated the sons of Adam, he set the bounds of the people according to the number of the children of Israel."* Deuteronomy 33:8

> *"...and hath determined the times before appointed, and the bounds of their habitation:"* Acts 17-26

God sets the boundaries of nations. God determines where people live, not governments. Nations are built around covenants and gods; not around political whims, international treaties, or the desire to make people feel better by transplanting them to other places around the globe.

When God created Israel, He was very specific about the immigration policies, and those who were to be allowed (or removed) within the nation. After all, they were established as one nation under God, and God instituted the policies that would keep them as such. They merely had to implement what He instituted. You will not hear most of this taught in churches today, because it deviates from the "group-hug" mentality, and the common-core Christianity that most pastors teach and embrace. It affects their finances, offends their congregations, and doesn't make people feel good. God will deal with these pastors, but in the meantime you should not support them with time, attendance, or finances. Immigration policy matters to God, and it needs to matter to you.

Three types of immigrants

There are three types of immigrant found in the Bible. They are: the legal immigrant, the illegal alien, and the refugee. Each group is treated differently in the Bible.

- Legal immigrants are required to adhere to the laws, language, religion and customs of the nation they enter. They do not come to colonize, they come to completely assimilate.
- Illegal immigrants are classified as invaders, and expelled.
- Refugees are allowed to remain for a period of time, and then either return to their own land or move to another land with laws and customs similar to their original land. They are required to adhere to the laws, language and religion of the land as well.

We don't hear about this today because globalists want to destroy nations. They want to blur the lines and make the world one huge mush-pot. They do this because polyglot cultures are not cohesive, and never develop the momentum of success. This allows them to retain power. God hates those that change the boundary lines of nations, or choose to ignore them. Hosea 5:10 tells us that He will pour out His wrath on people that try to do this.

Does God hate immigrants and refugees? No! Were all of them hated by God? Absolutely not. God said that His house would be called a house of prayer for all people. A multi*ethnic* nation is fine. However, God is absolutely opposed to a multi*cultural* nation. There is a difference...a BIG difference. The best definition of God's type of immigration is found in Ruth's declaration, when she told Naomi, *"thy people will be my people, and your God my God."* Ruth 1:16. Ruth was determined to completely assimilate.

How should illegal immigrants be handled?

Illegal immigrants should be expelled. Period. There now, that was easy.

- If you cross the North Korean border illegally you receive 12 years hard labor.
- If you cross the Iranian border illegally you are detained indefinitely.
- If you cross the Afghan border illegally you get shot.
- If you cross the Saudi Arabian border illegally you will be jailed.
- If you cross the Chinese border illegally you may never be heard from again.
- If you cross the Cuban border illegally you will be thrown into political prison to rot.

Immigration, God's way

What then are the terms and conditions of handling immigration in a biblical manner? Let's find out.

- Immigrants are to fear the God of the land and accept Him as their own. Numbers 15:30.
- Immigrants are to completely integrate into American culture and society. Ruth 1:16.

- Immigrants are to speak the national language. English only. Nehemiah 13:23-25.

- Immigrants are to observe the national and religious feasts of American culture. They are to cease from celebrating those from their former religions and heritage. Exodus 12:19

- Immigrants are to fully integrate into the Judeo-Christian faith, to make a house of prayer for all people. Isaiah 56:6-7.

- There are to be no government programs for immigrants. No welfare, housing, financial aid, etc. None! Leviticus 19:9-10.

- Any immigrant that brings in an abomination, such as homosexuality, idolatry, other religions, ancestral worship, or paganism is worthy of deportation or death. Leviticus 18:26.

- All immigrants must obey the same laws as the citizen. There are no special classes or privileges granted. Numbers 15:15-16.

- All illegal immigrants are deemed to be lawbreakers and are subject to immediate deportation. John 10:7-9.

- Immigrants are not to be vexed, but loved by the people of the land. They should not be made a subservient or oppressed class, but should be paid fairly based on the skills they offer. Leviticus 19:33-34.

- Immigrants should be received and loved by the citizens of the nation. Matthew 25:35.

Immigrants have been elevated to a special class in the United States, and have been given special government programs that are not available to the average American citizen. Paradoxically, they have also been exploited because of being a special class. This is evil, and must be stopped. It begins with a census, and must move forward from there.

There are three different aspects to immigration that must be addressed in order for policy to shift and benefit our nation.

The government

Today, government administers all immigration policy, and admits refugees, illegals and legal immigrants into the United States. Nehemiah began by building the wall. We should do the same, and close our borders. This creates a flow for immigration. Today the U.S. government does not seem to care when students from other nations simply do not go home when their visas expire. Government needs to deport them, and make sure they come and go in accordance with the law.

What else should the government do? The government must ensure that the immigrants that are brought in to America will adhere to the moral, religious, social and national fabric of America. All others are not welcome. If you are a muslim, you are not welcome here. If you want to cling to any other anti-Christian practice, go to another nation. This is not your society.

Government must help place immigrants into society so that they are fairly employed, *without receiving any subsistence from government*. It is up to the local communities, specifically the businesses and people, to help immigrants integrate into life and society. It is up to the immigrant to offer themselves as producers beneficial to our society, and fully embrace the national culture. All of the special programs, usually administered through fake charities, must stop. It is up to the area where the immigrant arrives to help that person adapt, find work, and learn to become a true American. If the immigrant cannot fit in, and cannot assimilate, the Federal government has no business trying to shove them down our throats. When the Federal government usurps local control, or engages in social engineering, it is overreaching its authority and must be neutered.

Government must apply the law equally to immigrants and citizens. If an immigrant breaks the law, or will not adhere to the moral and social structure of America, he or she should be deported. If a crime has been committed, it is up to the government to judge the crime and determine if that person is worthy of death or deportation. America must stop pandering to the globalists, and put teeth into her laws once again.

The immigrant

Every immigrant that arrives within our borders must understand his or her responsibilities that we outlined above. In Saudi Arabia, women must wear burkas. In many nations immigrants cannot own property. In New Guinea, it is nearly required that all citizens observe and respect Ramadan. It's time for immigrants to America to respect and uphold the God of the Bible, or they should be expelled. Immigrants should obey our laws, observe our customs, and forsake their old habits.

In January, 1919, former U.S. President Teddy Roosevelt said this: *"In the first place, we should insist that if the immigrant who comes here in good faith becomes an American and assimilates himself to us, he shall be treated on an exact equality with everyone else, for it is an outrage to discriminate against any such man because of creed, or birthplace, or origin. But this is predicated upon the person's becoming in every facet an American and nothing but an American. There can be no divided allegiance here. Any man who says he is an American, but something else also, isn't an American at all. We have room for but one flag, the American flag. We have room for but one language here, and that is the English language ... and we have room for but one sole loyalty and that is a loyalty to the American people."*

- Every immigrant should observe Christian and national U.S. holidays.
- Every immigrant must learn to speak English, and use that language to conduct business and operate in society.
- Every immigrant must know and abide by the laws of our Judeo-Christian nation.
- Every immigrant must learn about Christianity, and live life under its precepts.

These were the standards that were set forth by Almighty God for His covenant people. This does not require immigrants to convert, but if they want to live here it does require them to live by the framework upon which our nation exists. Whether-or-not they convert is between them and God. But whether-or-not they attempt to colonize vs. assimilate is between them and us. God has delegated His regulations to us as a nation under God, and it is up to us to implement.

The citizen

God commanded the citizens to be tenderhearted toward the legal immigrant and the refugee. God reminded them that they were once strangers in Egypt, and Pharaoh treated them kindly (at first). Too many times, immigrants have been brought into America only as a form of cheap labor, or a people that can be manipulated or oppressed. This is evil in God's sight. It robs from the immigrant, and it also robs from the citizens by taking job opportunities away from them.

In the book of Ruth we observe that Boaz employed Ruth as an immigrant, and he paid her as well as he would have a citizen. God commanded repeatedly that the citizen was to love the immigrant and receive them. If there were no government programs or special assistance, it would be up to the local citizen, business and other groups to minister to the immigrant. Once again, we see how the shift of charity from the government to the churches would connect the immigrant to God as a source, instead of connecting them to the State which wants to play hero. It worked then. It will work now.

Nehemiah and the people of Judah were committed to building a great nation. They were building one nation under One God. The census was a strategic part of that commitment, because it helped determine who belonged, and who did not. They had to know who was committed to the land; they had to be selective in who stayed, and who must go. As a nation in covenant with God, they could afford to be picky. God's blessings were on the way, and the world community could not be allowed to suck the life out of the nation. America must similarly reform immigration policy if she wants to be great again.

> *Verily, verily, I say unto you, He that entereth not by the door into the sheepfold, but climbeth up some other way, the same is a thief and a robber. I am the door: by me if any man enter in, he shall be saved, and shall go in and out, and find pasture.*
> John 10:1,9

Rule #11: Institute Bible-based immigration practices.

Questions:

- If you are a bleeding heart globalist, how do you need to change?
- What needs to change in U.S. immigration policy? How can you help change it?
- What kinds of foreigners need to be expelled from the U.S.?

Chapter 12 - Church on the Wall

Nehemiah 12

Here are the rules up to this point:

Rule 1:   Repent, and determine to become one nation under One God. Repentance is the foundation, the key ingredient to make America great again. We must get honest, we must get real, we must depart from the globalist mindset we currently love and embrace.

Rule 2:   Reject globalism, reject the status quo, and identify the enemies within America. There are great enemies of American exceptionalism and liberty at work within our borders. They must be recognized as such, and must be opposed and defeated.

Rule 3:   Embrace nationalism under God, and get involved. Build that wall!

Rule 4:   Keep and bear arms. Prepare to defend American liberty and exceptionalism with deadly force. The people's right to keep and bear arms is necessary for the survival of a free people. There are no bad guns; only bad hearted people that may use guns. They need to be dealt with, and swiftly.

Rule 5:   Abandon the global economy and its commonly accepted practices. Return to a wealth-based, biblically founded national economy.

Rule 6: Refuse to be intimidated, take the initiative and go on the offense. Government must be of the people, by the people and for the people.

Rule 7: Tighten the screws on commerce and leadership eligibility. No outsourcing, no foreigners in positions of power.

Rule 8: Make the Holy Bible the common law of the United States of America. Every other law and statute must conform to it, or be rendered invalid.

Rule 9: Reclaim America's History! It must be restored to be Judeo-Christian in heritage and worldview!

Rule 10: Separate social programs and charitable spending from government.

Rule 11: Institute Bible-based immigration practices.

Nehemiah 12 begins with another list; a list of priests and ministers in Jerusalem. It also provides us with the twelfth rule for rebuilders.

The state of the Union

For Judah and Jerusalem, the government, citizenry, and church are now in harmony with Almighty God's agenda for the nation. It is time for them to dedicate their completed border security operation (the wall), and celebrate the death of globalism! If there's something worth celebrating, this is it! After all, this is Jerusalem's 4th of July moment, in which they celebrate their independence, liberty, and God-given possessions and rights. For the FIRST TIME in that generation's history, they are a free people, and they celebrate by giving thanks to, and worshiping Almighty God alone.

Comparing it to American holidays, Jerusalem's celebration is like Thanksgiving, Christmas, and the 4th of July wrapped up into one event. Though we separate them into distinct holidays in our time, they are all conjoined in purpose and foundation. John Quincy Adams, sixth president of the United States, noted a fact about the beginning of the United States of America. On July 4, 1837 he said, *"Why is it that, next to the birthday of the Savior of the World, your most joyous and most venerated festival returns on this day? . . . Is it not that, in the chain of human events, the birthday of the nation is indissolubly linked with the birthday of the Savior? That it forms a leading event in the progress of the Gospel dispensation? Is it not that the Declaration of Independence first organized the social compact on the foundation of the Redeemer's mission upon earth? That it laid the cornerstone of human government upon the first precepts of Christianity, and gave to the world the first irrevocable pledge of the fulfillment of the prophecies, announced directly from Heaven at the birth of the Savior and predicted by the greatest of the Hebrew prophets six hundred years before?"*

In Judah's history, this is literally one of their greatest moments, and now it is time to worship the one true God who made it all possible. It is time to have a church service to worship and celebrate.

Worship on the wall

When it was time to dedicate the wall, the State...yes, the State...sought out the church for the dedication service. The two are seen working in complete harmony with each other, moving hand in hand. Separate functions, one purpose.

Was the service a neatly polished one-hour production, complete with an espresso bar, flashing stage lights, and dim sanctuary lighting? No.

Was the service programmed to the minute, complete with a cool PowerPoint presentation? No.

Was the service led by a cute metrosexual with facial hair, wearing a t-shirt, skinny jeans, and sporting a new "I Have A Past" tattoo? No.

Was the service "seeker sensitive," catering to all the elements of the culture? No.

Was the service held in the temple, a nice atmosphere conducive to worship? No.

Daily services were held in the temple, on an ongoing basis. But THIS service, the worship service for the dedication of the wall, was held...on the wall! No espresso, no fog machine, no PowerPoint slides, no organ music, no glitz, no glamor. But there were plenty of men with swords. Prepared for battle. Prepared for true worship. Prepared to kick butt.

This was a national act of worship, sponsored by the State... and ministers, educators, musicians, and warriors came together from across the entire nation to take part in this dedication.

On. The. Wall.

The service began at the gate which was furthest from the temple itself; the dung gate. Make sure you get that. The greatest worship service in history did not start in a church building, it ended there.

From the dung gate, other musicians, singers, and ministers spread completely around the city, standing on the walls with trumpets, Scriptures and songs. The soldiers and watchmen remained on the wall to be blessed by the ministers. The trumpets blasted over the city, and songs of praise were sung. Prayers were prayed and Scriptures read over the wall. This was their national service of celebration and dedication.

On. The. Wall.

Let's talk about (your) church

If your church was invited by the President, to conduct a dedication service on the newly-built border security wall between Mexico and these United States, how many in your church congregation would attend? Would your pastor have the strength to lead the effort, or would it be too controversial for him? How many of your congregation would be offended? Would it upset your community outreach goals, or your denominational headquarters? How many would be upset, standing by an armed guard with shoot-to-kill orders against any illegal or invader that sought to breach the wall? How many would demonstrate against the closed-minded views of this government? How many would prefer a good potluck instead, followed by a vote to select carpet colors for the sanctuary?

If this describes your church, why are you still attending?

Let us help put this in perspective:

Islam is invading America, soon to replace Judaism as the number two religion here. Christianity hangs by a thread as number one. Meanwhile, illegal immigrants and terrorists pour across our borders with one unified agenda; destroy America as it exists today. The enemy within (in both parties) has united with the U.N. and global interests to destroy American sovereignty. And all you want is a feel-good church setting?

Please don't tell us you attend the First Church of Potlucks because of their fabulous glorified daycare programs for irresponsible parents (aka "children's ministries").

Please don't tell us you attend the big box church of the Holy Fog Machine because of their fabulous dating opportunities (aka "singles ministries").

For crying out loud, join an Internet dating site, and find a church that is willing to worship on the wall! You may want to put that in your online dating profile as well.

If you belong to a church that is majoring in minors, leave! Now! These people are the ones that try to adapt God to their point of view, instead of conforming to His viewpoint. The prophet Jeremiah lamented over Judah in another era because of this mindset. His words in Jeremiah 5:31 ring as true today as they did back then.

The prophets prophesy falsely, and the priests bear rule by their means; and my people love to have it so: and what will ye do in the end thereof?

Does that describe you? Your church?

The church in Nehemiah's day was only effective insofar as it was willing to build THE kingdom...not its OWN kingdom. In many ways, the modern American church has become a kingdom unto itself, and is content to function within its own four walls. It is not willing to get on the wall, and has embraced a picture of Jesus that is wholly unscriptural. They present a Jesus who is nicer than Jesus; one who would never make a whip and cleanse the temple with violence. One who would never say a harsh word. One who only gives hugs. They want God to be a globalist, and errantly believe that a "coexist" bumper sticker will stick to the backside of a camel. They want God to stop being so rigid. They are NOT followers of God, but by idolizing other cultures they are trying to make Him into a servant that they can manipulate and control. Just like the Pharisees in Jesus' day. They killed Jesus, by the way.

The church in Nehemiah's time sported freshly printed "Overcome" bumper stickers! They took their AR-15's to church. They were not obsessed with climate change, because they actually BELIEVED God's covenant promise in Genesis 8:22 (read it, it will not fail). They understood that God had not judged them because they did not recycle, but had judged them for embracing globalism, cultural equivalency, and religious equivalency.

Truth is not relative

There was no allowance in the church on the wall for creating your own truth. If you were a part of this service and this congregation, you embraced God's agenda. Period. The only God that was worshipped by the nation was Almighty God Himself. There were no coexist bumper stickers in the church parking lot!

- No Buddha.
- No Mohammed.
- No Krishna.
- No Gaia.
- No celebrations of diversity or perversity.
- No multicultural "we are the world" tolerant crap.

Only Almighty God. The God of Abraham, Isaac, Jacob. The God of the Bible. Period. He is the God of the city and the nation, and every other god is subservient or cast out.

National policies and politics also reflect the harmony between church and State.

- Education is now rooted in Christianity; not government.
- The economy has been reformed into a wealth-based system instead of relying on debt.
- Border security and national stability are now a reality.

Not JUST because of a wall...but because of ALL their reforms AND the wall.

In short, this was no wimpy church. They were national in viewpoint; not global. They stood with the military and law enforcement. It was full of masculinity, strength, and power. They sang on the wall, and praised God for their liberty and sovereignty. They praised God that globalism and multiculturalism were dead. They praised God for this wall that represented His work in their nation. They praised God, armed to the teeth.

Retooling our focus

This may come as a shock to some, but God has not changed one iota since Nehemiah's day. God did not take a Prozac at the end of Malachi, and become the drooling grandpa that many think He is today. He is the same yesterday, today, and forever, and He is still the One God, for this "one nation UNDER God." God wasn't interested in national affairs in the Old Testament, only to become disinterested in them today. Having read the Bible cover to cover several times, nowhere have we found the phrase "Oops, saith the Lord." God is equally interested in the affairs of America today, as He was in Judah in Nehemiah's time.

Unfortunately, the modern American church has taken America too lightly. We read the words of Jesus to "go into the all the world," and assume that America is the starting point for that endeavor. In truth, America is the end game for that endeavor. In Acts 1, when Jesus instructed His followers to start in Jerusalem, work outward to Judea and Samaria, and end things in the "uttermost part of the earth," Jesus was using Jerusalem as the starting point. The "uttermost part" is the furthest possible land mass from that location, which is the western states of the United States. America is the end game! America is liberty's last stand! If we lose Zimbabwe to tyrants, we lose Zimbabwe. If we lose America to tyrants, we lose the entire globe to tyranny! America is the final Christian frontier, and cannot be lost to the enemy. There is nowhere left to colonize "for the glory of God, and advancement of the Christian faith." This nation called America is a big deal to God, yet American Christians almost treat it as an afterthought. The American church pours its emphasis and resources into foreign missions. It congratulates itself for its effort, then has a potluck while America goes to hell.

The modern American church has been feminized, sanitized and neutered. Strength has been taken from the church, and evangelism has been deified over kingdom. In America, the church has been turned into a hospital instead of an army. The church enables the weak instead of training for strength. The church has coddled sin instead of standing for holiness and purity. The church has ignored its role in shaping government, while begging for self-serving escapism, so that they don't have to endure any fires of affliction that will purify and refine. No wonder America is in the state that it is in.

To build America, the church must conform to God and to His Bible once again. The church cannot continue to ignore or excuse Scripture rather than wrestling with it and choosing to obey what it says. All of it! In addition, the church can no longer make itself the object of its work, but must retool its focus to line up with God's agenda. Think of it this way; if a builder wants to build a house, he has an assortment of tools that he uses to accomplish the task. The house is the goal, and the tools are simply instruments to accomplish the goal. A hammer does not exist to make itself into a prettier hammer. The builder does not use the hammer to build the hammer, he uses it to build something bigger than the hammer. The house is the object, the hammer is the tool. The church is God's tool, not God's object. The object is the kingdom...on earth, as it is in heaven. America does not need Christian narcissists; it needs Christian patriots, willing to get out of their safe spaces, and worship on the wall.

We cannot have a spiritual awakening without physical work, and a focus larger than ourselves. The modern American church cannot have a spiritual revival without reforming society according to the rules in Nehemiah. When the church gets serious about instituting these rules to change America, then (and only then) will the church experience the true revival it is praying for.

- The church cannot have revival without repentance.
- The church cannot have revival without taking responsibility for her part in enabling the sins of the nation.
- The church cannot have revival without repenting of her laziness in civic duty.
- The church cannot have revival without enforcing border security.
- The church cannot have revival without returning the economy to God's hands.
- The church cannot have revival while she ignores or denies what God says about national issues.
- The church cannot have revival by living a pacifist lifestyle.
- The church cannot have revival without taking responsibility for the breakdown of the rule of law, and propping up sanctuary cities.

The local church congregation we pastor joyfully sings a song that was written by one of the men in the church, Greg Worrell. It is called "The Warrior Song."

We sing the warrior song, and pray we do no wrong,
Grace is God's enabling power.
We sing the warrior song, and pray we do no wrong,
Make us mighty men of valor.

For those of you that are more seasoned in the hymns, you may remember this song.

Onward! Christian soldiers. Marching as to war,
With the cross of Jesus going on before.
Christ the Royal Master leads against the foe.

Forward into battle, see His banners go.
Onward! Christian soldiers. Marching as to war,
With the cross of Jesus going on before.

Revival never began with a song like "Onward Christian Pacifists." Revival begins when the church turns its heart to God's way of dealing with national issues.

> *"Let the priests, the ministers of the Lord, weep between the porch and the altar, and let them say, Spare thy people, O Lord, and give not thine heritage to reproach, that the heathen should rule over them: wherefore should they say among the people, Where is their God? Then will the Lord be jealous for his land, and pity his people."* Joel 2:17-18

A companion book to Nehemiah is the book of Ezra. It was written from the perspective of Ezra the priest, who led the first group back to the broken down city of Jerusalem. That group began working on the temple, long before the city walls were built by Nehemiah. Ezra spent more than 50 years trying to rebuild the temple. He successfully instituted worship of Almighty God, but had little impact on the overall culture of Jerusalem until Nehemiah came on the scene. The revival of Jerusalem came when the church helped to build the wall and reform society. Then, and only then, was true worship rekindled in Jerusalem. Revival in the church happens when the church starts to obey God's Word and patterns again.

A homogenous culture

By the time this celebration was done in Nehemiah 12, the boundaries between faith and State were clear. Only one faith was accepted to govern the nation; it was one nation under One God.

Only one faith was allowed in schools. The tribe of Levi taught the Bible in school. Only one faith was used in the dedication of the wall. It was the faith of Almighty God alone. The Bible was the common law of the nation. The church was the place of worship toward Almighty God. The nation was in unity, and church and State were in one accord.

Because of the unity, the blessing of God flowed. The tithes and giving flowed into the church, to provide for the ministers and also to be used for charity. There was great abundance in the church *and* in the State. Now the wall built by the State was dedicated to God Himself. One nation, under One God.

The end result? The culture was completely homogenized. The reader of Nehemiah 12 may find it difficult given the lengthy list of names, but notice that they're all names of natural born Judah-ites. The nation has returned to its founding culture, and the foreign controls over Judah are now a thing of the past.

> *And their nobles shall be of themselves, and their governor shall proceed from the midst of them; and I will cause him to draw near, and he shall approach unto me: for who is this that engaged his heart to approach unto me? saith the Lord...* Jeremiah 30:21

Rule #12: Develop a kingdom and warrior mindset. No more wimpy church!

Questions:

- Would you worship at church on the wall, or protest the action?
- What do you need to do, to realign your mindset about God's ways?
- Do you worship at a culturally relevant, tolerant, multi-cultural church? Repent! Leave!

Chapter 13 - Unfinished Business

Nehemiah 13

There are twelve rules drawn from Nehemiah that we have given you; one for each chapter we have studied. They cover religion, economics, border security, the right to keep and bear arms, and more. It's the start that stops most people, but finishing well can also prove to be difficult. Nation building outside of global control requires resolve and follow through, especially once the imminent threats to national sovereignty have been overcome. *The work must be finished.* Nehemiah's closing actions are a testament to that, and also a challenge to our generation. In this chapter we will give you the final rule for rebuilders. As we have stated throughout this entire book, it worked in Nehemiah's day, and will work in America today.

Nehemiah

The walls are built, the economy is humming, and government infrastructure is lean and operating well. The local synagogues are full, and the churches are running the schools, charities and a host of civic organizations. The border security wall has been dedicated, and the churches, pastors and congregations of the nation have led the national celebration. The people have repented before God, and are once again committed to doing what He commands. They want to BE one nation under One God; not just say it. They want the God of the blessing, not just the blessing of God. Therein lies the key to national exceptionalism and sovereignty, in the face of a global beast that abhors their liberty. In short, life in Jerusalem is great again, and the global system has not been given a say in her affairs.

But in the background a problem lurks, brooding, scheming. It has to be dealt with if Jerusalem is going to remain viable and free. There is more to be done, and Nehemiah has to act. Decisively.

His actions will provide us with our final rule for rebuilders.

Tobiah

Tobiah, the personification of the enemy within, has been secretly enraged at the changes made in Jerusalem. You may remember him from chapters 2 and 3 as one of the influential subversives that controlled things before Nehemiah's appearance on the scene. He tried repeatedly to undermine Nehemiah and every patriot in the nation. At first his defiance was overt, but as nationalism has taken hold, he has become more covert. But like a bad virus, he is still there. He is a true progressive, and he likes the old Jerusalem that was under global control. Tobiah has been mooching off the system and corrupting it for his own benefit.

But he hasn't been acting alone. Who was helping him, and colluding with him against Nehemiah and the government? The corrupt and progressive church! The pastors of some of the influential churches, and those that held the purse strings, kept Tobiah well-fed, clothed and housed in a veritable palace. The enemies within are not limited to government, but they are always in collusion with the global system. Many of them are pseudo-religious leaders. In fact, some may pastor churches you know and attend. But now, he and his circle of influential friends and associates have slowly lost power, money and status with the locals. Some have left town, and given up on their progressive agenda. But Tobiah has not left. He is waiting for the next administration, the next wave of globalists to rise up and seize power again, because government usually operates on a pendulum. He is counting on this, to make his move. Until then he lurks in the shadows.

The resolve of free men will always be tested.

Enemies foreign and domestic

God specifically listed several groups in the Bible that were not allowed to be a part of God's chosen people. Deuteronomy provides a grocery list.

- The Ammonites and Moabites.
- The inhabitants of the land that will not cooperate with God's chosen people.
- Immigrants that will not adhere to God's standards and worship.
- Illegal aliens and foreign intruders.
- Those that rebel against God and want to change His nation.
- Those that seek to consume from the nation without fully assimilating.

All of these people were "persona non grata." They were not welcome in the nation that sought to be one nation under One God.

These nations and people had actively worked to overthrow and subert Israel. They were banned from entering the House of Judah. Forever.

Nehemiah had built a wall. He had appointed the leadership. He had taken the census. Now it was time to put it all to work. By verse 3, they began by separating ALL "the mixed multitude" from Israel.

- Did the church try to evangelize them? No.
- Did the schools try to teach them English? Not anymore.
- Did the local cultural centers teach the citizens how to relate to these people? Not now.
- Did the local charities try to drum up assistance for these families? No.

The fruit of national worship did not involve evangelism. It involved separation. This is an inconvenient truth to most churches and pastors, because they have deified evangelism, and are using it to build their kingdom, not THE kingdom. They have embraced globalism, and no longer stand in defense of our nation. They have used national policy to justify what they want the Bible to say, instead of obeying what it does say. Now the line is drawn in the sand, and Nehemiah's message to them is simple; get out.

Cue the weeping and gnashing of teeth by the bad guys.

- What if these people had children born in the nation? Throw them out.
- What if they wanted to be here so that they could have a good life? Throw them out.
- What if they were of the same race as a family member? Throw them out.
- What if they had been here for twenty years? Throw them out.
- What if they didn't want to go? Throw them out.
- What if they were nice? Throw them out.

Throw. Them. Out!
Cue the rejoicing by the saints.

Throw out the dreamers

As we write this book there is a debate raging about how to address several categories of people. There are the families that have "anchor babies," babies that are born in America that give the family a free pass to migrate to America. There are other families that bring in children that were born in other nations, but have now lived much of their life in America. Still others have overstayed student visas and have remained. Illegals have stolen identities, taken jobs, and embedded themselves into life and society. But the vast majority of these people have one thing in common. They don't care about the nation. They only care about themselves. They are not dreaming the American dream, they are dreaming their own dream. One man's dream can be a national nightmare.

On January 20, 1961, in his inaugural address the late President John F. Kennedy said, *"Ask not what your country can do for you, but what you can do for your country."* God does not build a great nation around self-serving people. He can only build around people that serve God.

Luke 19 tells the story of the investments of three men. One had invested one pound, and gained back ten pounds. The second invested one pound and gained five. The third took the pound given to him, and did not invest it. He did nothing productive, yet still wanted God to honor him and care for him. When the master returned, he honored the first two servants and removed the third. Luke 19:26 tells the rest of the story.

> *"For I say unto you, That unto every one which hath shall be given; and from him that hath not, even that he hath shall be taken away from him."* Luke 19:26

If you haven't already done so, you can stick a fork in the notion that God is a socialist. You still reap what you sow, and equal outcome is not a scriptural principle. Equal opportunity? Yes. Equal outcome? No.

Bleeding heart liberals can't wrap their heads around the fact that God...GOD...will take resources from lazy consumers, and give them to industrious producers. The reasons are really simple, though they don't sit well with the enemies of national exceptionalism. In this parable, the lazy consumer refused to acknowledge that he was accountable to something greater than himself, and he was to invest in THAT...not just HIM. He was to be productive in life, society, and in a realm greater than himself. He sought only to preserve himself; he invested only for self, and expected the master to conform to his laziness.

Much like Tobiah was doing with national resources in Nehemiah's day.

Much like the dreamers do with national resources today.

They do nothing to advance the good of the kingdom, and exist in America only for themselves. And they expect the prevailing culture within America to adapt...to them. God will not rebuild America upon self-centered, self-serving, self-promoting people.

Throw. Them. Out.

When an immigrant comes into America, they must seek to make AMERICA great. They must put country before self, they must come as producers, not leeches. They must be determined to fully assimilate upward to the founding culture of America, and become an American in every sense of the word. America will be rebuilt as a multi-ethnic nation, but she must be mono-cultural. One nation. One God. As for the rest?

Throw. Them. Out.

Self-interested and self-serving

You can frequently recognize the enemy within by observing one key trait. They are more interested in consolidating and protecting their power than the liberties of the people. They get away with it, simply because they can. They can be found in government, the church, business, the media, entertainment, and education. Nehemiah's absence and inability (to this point) to address necessary issues in government allowed Tobiah and the domestic terrorists with him to coexist. Now it's time to rip that bumper sticker off their horses, and deal with them. What was the solution? Get back in the saddle and throw the bums out! This is precisely what Nehemiah did in verse 9.

The final step of the spiritual revival in Judah was this: identify the enemy within...and throw them out!

America...the day will come when we throw the bums out! That day *must* come! Every dreamer. Every illegal. Every self-serving refugee. Every foreign interest that works against America. Every pastor that collaborates or provides sanctuary for this treason. They obviously hate a nationalistic America, and would do better somewhere else, in a culture that caters to them being a privileged class. Help them leave, pay for their (one way) plane ticket even.

Throw. Them. Out.

But wait! There's more!

The rest of Nehemiah 13 deals with enforcement. Most of the nation is resolved to *enforce* the laws that are in place. There is no need for new laws, when the old laws will suffice. Now, action must be taken at many levels.

Nehemiah chose to begin with enforcement...in the church! Not only did Nehemiah deport all of the dreamers, but he threw Eliashib (the priest that supported Tobiah the globalist insurgent) out of leadership! He fired him!

Then Nehemiah began to deal with the bureaucrats in government again. Apparently they weren't implementing the laws that had been enacted in chapter 10, separating government from charity. Nehemiah set them in *their* place! He brought in new treasurers, recruited from the churches because they were men of integrity and would be faithful to the God-fearing laws that had been implemented. As for the old, entrenched bureaucrats? Nehemiah fired them too.

Nehemiah did all of this for a singular purpose, that is revealed repeatedly in this closing chapter. It was for the glory of God, not the accolades of foreign powers.

> *"Remember me, O my God, concerning this, and wipe not out my good deeds that I have done for the house of my God, and for the offices thereof."*
> Nehemiah 13:14

God takes note of what we do with our national affairs. Several verses in this chapter show that Nehemiah appealed directly to heaven, and requested that God recognize him for his efforts in government. This is where God and government come together.

Blue laws

Finally Nehemiah dealt with two closing issues. The first was the restoration of a law that had been ignored for years. It was the law of the Sabbath. For years, the nation had claimed to worship God while ignoring Him. Some may have attended church. Some may have influenced their families in a godly way. Some may have wanted to turn back the clock, but nobody did. Until Nehemiah. He was the catalyst willing to take risks of faith in government, so that God would be blessed by the nation. This opened the door for God to bless the nation in return.

Laws and decisions ALWAYS have unintended consequences. Progressives continually magnify the anomalies or failures of the founding culture so they can manipulate it. They don't give credence to any position that balances out the argument, because they are not seeking balance...they are seeking offense. Once offended enough, they can then dictate the terms of surrender to the winners who established the culture to begin with. This is their tactic to swing things farther to the left, whether immediately or eventually. Conservatives and Christians feel that guilt, and distrust the unknown and/or bold action, and consequently fail to take strong, bold steps of faith. They know intuitively that bold steps are needed, but fear the anomalies and failures that will occur. Hence, they are paralyzed from doing anything, and eventually overcome. It is time for Christians to do what God commands, and trust Him with the outcome. The commands are His, and the consequences will be His to ordain, too.

What did Nehemiah do that was bold? He instituted a national Sabbath day for the entire nation. This had been done in the past, but had been abandoned. Under Nehemiah, all trade, all commerce, even most travel ceased throughout the nation.

Nehemiah instituted penalties for those that ignored the national Sabbath day. He forced the merchants from other nations to stop selling on the Sabbath, and even forbade them from camping around the city walls (to entice people out to buy on the Sabbath). The laws of God were becoming the laws of the state once again.

English only

Nehemiah also recognized the intentionally blurred lines that globalism had created in language, culture, and intermarriage. Verse 24 shows that many of the children did not speak the language of the land, and that intermarriage had weakened the national fabric of the nation. Scripture shows us (verse 25) that Nehemiah literally cursed these people, beat some of them, and chased them out! They had defiled the land, and were not to be tolerated. The focus was to be the kingdom of God; not the culture of man.

Thus, we conclude the story of national renewal under Nehemiah.

For Nehemiah the renewal effort is done. For America, it has yet to begin. God is looking for you to stand in this generation as a Nehemiah. You. Yes, you. Get ready to throw the bums out.

For it shall come to pass in that day, saith the Lord of hosts, that I will break his yoke from off thy neck, and will burst thy bonds, and strangers shall no more serve themselves of him. Jeremiah 30:8

Rule #13: Throw the bums out. English only. One nation; One God.

Questions:

- Are you comfortable deporting Dreamers, illegal aliens and other seditious people from the United States? What other commands of God do you resist?
- Would you be willing to serve in government and enforce the laws of God?
- Will you work to bring these rules back to America? Where will you begin?

Conclusion

"Remember me, O my God, for good."

The closing line of the book of Nehemiah provides the motivation that drove Nehemiah. He abandoned a powerful, stable career so that he could restore and rebuild Jerusalem. God helped Nehemiah, but he and those around him did the work.

Today, many of the walls of Jerusalem are still standing, 2,500 years later, because Nehemiah and the others listed in the book were willing to work. What will you build? Who will you collaborate with? What will you do?

The rules we have laid out in this book are not our own; they are God's rules. You can try to build America based on other rules, but you will fail. Hasn't history already shown that to be the case?

Let's be clear; we have a simple and unified message, about America, for all subversives:

- For muslims;
- For buddhists;
- For communists;
- For socialists;
- For #blacklivesmatter;
- For antifa;
- For illegals;
- For foreign governments;
- For globalists;

- For atheists;
- For squishy Christians;
- For the mainstream media;
- For democrats;
- For republicans;
- And for every other enemy of America;

Our message to them, about America?
You didn't build that.

We don't intend to let them redefine our nation into their image. The field belongs to God and His people, and their only smart option is to get on His side. It is just a matter of time before globalism and progressivism lose the fight, so surrender now.

When we do things our way, we fail every time. In Romans 10 the apostle Paul talks about people that want to do things their own way.

> *"For they being ignorant of God's righteousness, and going about to establish their own righteousness, have not submitted themselves unto the righteousness of God."* Romans 10:3

Your way? Or God's way.

When Jesus Christ taught His disciples to pray, he instructed us to use the template He provided in Matthew 6.

> *"Thy kingdom come, Thy will be done in earth, as it is in heaven."* Matthew 6:10

We have spent far too much time expecting God to work in heaven, based on what we have on earth. It's time to reverse that. It's time to bring the kingdom of heaven mindset, authority and rules to earth once again. In our personal lives. In our families. In our cities. And in the United States of America.

You should not be asking whether God wants to use you. You need to ask how and where God intends to place you in this fight. Make no mistake, it will be a battle. Globalists will hate you. You will be demonized by society around you. Nobody said it would be easy, but with God all things are possible. Will you believe?

As we close this chapter, a new one opens. It will be written by you, by God, and by your friends and allies. It's time for the patriots in America to repent and embrace God's rules. And once again, it's time to get to work.

You may be discouraged by what you see in society. We understand. But like God told Elijah the prophet when he thought he was the only one left, there are many more around you than you realize. It's up to you to find them.

As we penned this book, it was a labor of love.

- Love for God.
- Love for the Bible, God's Word.
- Love for America.
- Love for God's heritage.
- Love for God's people.

Several heroes of faith are already involved in the fight with us. Destiny Christian Center has been involved in bringing America back to God for several years. We love and thank them for their strength and support. There are others! To those that read through the manuscript, chapter-by-chapter, as it was being put onto paper:

- To Jennifer;
- To Toy;
- To Geoff and Erin;
- To Rusty and Katie;
- To Glenda;

- To Ben and Sarah;
- To Elisabeth;
- To Steve and Becky;
- To Mike and Marsha;
- To Jan;

And to a host of unnamed heroes, we salute you.

This is how America is to be made great again. Be under no illusion: things are going to get worse, before they get better. History holds a special spot for the underdog who comes back in the bottom of the 9th. You never hear the story of Ted vs. Joe, but the story of David vs. Goliath is known around the world. That's because Ted and Joe were evenly matched :-). When the little guy, the good guy, wins...against overwhelming odds...it warms the spirit of other good guys.

Taking on tyrants. It's what God made us to do.

Let's begin. Now.

Are you in?

> *"...For Thine is the kingdom, and the power, and the glory, for ever. Amen.* Matthew 6:13

Rules for Rebuilders

Rule 1:   Repent, and determine to become one nation under One God. Repentance is the foundation, the key ingredient to make America great again. We must get honest, we must get real, we must depart from the globalist mindset we currently love and embrace.

Rule 2:   Reject globalism, reject the status quo, and identify the enemies within America. There are great enemies of American exceptionalism and liberty at work within our borders. They must be recognized as such, and must be opposed and defeated.

Rule 3:   Embrace nationalism under God, and get involved. Build that wall!

Rule 4:   Keep and bear arms. Prepare to defend American liberty and exceptionalism with deadly force. The people's right to keep and bear arms is necessary for the survival of a free people. There are no bad guns; only bad hearted people that may use guns. They need to be dealt with, and swiftly.

Rule 5:   Abandon the global economy and its commonly accepted practices. Return to a wealth-based, biblically founded national economy.

Rule 6:   Refuse to be intimidated, take the initiative and go on the offense. Government must be of the people, by the people and for the people.

Rule 7:   Tighten the screws on commerce and leadership eligibility. No outsourcing, no foreigners in positions of power.

Rule 8:   Make the Holy Bible the common law of the United States of America. Every other law and statute must conform to it, or be rendered invalid.

Rule 9:   Reclaim America's History! It must be restored to be Judeo-Christian in heritage and worldview!

Rule 10: Separate social programs and charitable spending from government.

Rule 11: Institute Bible-based immigration practices.

Rule 12: Develop a kingdom and warrior mindset. No more wimpy church!

Rule 13: Throw the bums out. English only. One nation; One God.

Remember me, O my God, for good.

About the Authors

Steven Grant is a pastor, author, and musician.

Stanley Grant is an author, talk show host, speaker, and Christian patriot.

Together, they are working to rebuild the United States of America for the glory of God and the advancement of the Christian faith.